# That's Such A God Thing

*Looking for God's Miracles Daily*

HELEN McLEOD ROGERS

WESTBOW
PRESS®
A DIVISION OF THOMAS NELSON
& ZONDERVAN

The author of God Loves You Better Than Mac and
Cheese has released this second book.

Scripture taken from the King James Version of the Bible.

WestBow Press books may be ordered through booksellers or by contacting:

WestBow Press
A Division of Thomas Nelson & Zondervan
1663 Liberty Drive
Bloomington, IN 47403
www.westbowpress.com
1 (866) 928-1240

ISBN: 978-1-5127-1542-2 (sc)
ISBN: 978-1-5127-1543-9 (hc)
ISBN: 978-1-5127-1541-5 (e)

Library of Congress Control Number: 2015916639

Print information available on the last page.

WestBow Press rev. date: 10/22/2015

## Dedication Page

Thank you to my wonderful husband Ed Rogers of 45 years.
He is the most loving, and caring man I know. He helps me
to get to all my speaking engagements without getting lost.
This book is for my precious children Marsha, Dawn, Tom,
Tim, Jeff, and Susie. I am blessed with a precious daughter-in-
law named Laney and a wonderful son-in-law named Kelvin.
I love my precious grandchildren: Heidi, Kassi, Cole, Tori,
and Emmaline, you are all precious miracles from God. I
dedicate this book to my sweet sisters, Marilyn and Sue and
in memory of our parents Thomas and Mary McLeod who
raised us in the Lord. Many thanks go to Katie for typing
this book. Thank you Jesus for being my Lord and Savior, for
allowing me to be Your child, and to work in Your kingdom.

About The Cover: On the front of this book are my precious
grandchildren; all miracles from the Lord. Each child
is different and unique. God has a special plan for each
one. We took over 200 pictures trying to get five unique
individuals to look at the camera at the same time!

These stories are true but the names and places are
changed to protect the identity of the individuals.

# Table of Contents

# 1

## Lisa and the Twins

"For I know the thoughts that I think toward you, saith the Lord, thoughts of peace, and not of evil, to give you an expected end." Jeremiah 29:11 (KJV)

I am the director of several crisis pregnancy centers. I get calls all the time from women who are looking for abortions. One day I received a call from Lisa (not her real name). She asked, "Do you have a two-for-one sale for abortions? I am pregnant with twin girls." I said that we didn't do abortions or refer for abortions, but please don't hang up on me; let's talk. Lisa said she already had an appointment for Thursday at 10:00 a.m. She agreed to come in to talk to me. I met with her, and I didn't talk about the babies. I asked about Lisa.

Her story was a sad and lonely one. Her family had told her everyday of her life that she was ugly and a mistake. They also told her that it would have been better if Lisa had been aborted and that was the reason Lisa's dad had left. Lisa saw herself as worthless, only to be used. I shared with Lisa how much Jesus loved her and that she was a beautiful creation of God. We talked, and she said she was going to keep her appointment on Thursday to abort her babies. I had prayer with Lisa and asked God to intervene by letting her have four flat tires on Thursday or that the abortion clinic would not accept her insurance on Thursday. I called all the prayer warriors and asked them to pray.

Thursday came, and we prayed. I called her at 12:00 p.m. to see how she was doing. She sounded happy. She shared with me that the abortion clinic would not take her insurance, even though it had been approved the week before. Lisa agreed to come in the next week. I kept praying. Lisa came in the next week and confessed that she had gone out-of-town to try to get an abortion. She had carried $1000 in cash hoping to get the abortion that day. The abortionist took one look at Lisa and said, "You are one day too late for an abortion." You have to know that was a God Moment, most abortionists don't tell you that you are one day too late.

We know that abortionists do what they do for the money. Lisa looked at me and said, "Miss Helen, this Jesus you talked about seems to be getting in my way." I told her that Jesus loved her and that He was trying to protect her and her little girls.

After that, Lisa started coming to the center. A local church adopted her and her precious girls. The church gave her a baby shower and money to help with her bills while she was out on maternity leave. The girls are beautiful, and Lisa is a good mother. She has accepted Jesus and has gone back to school to get her license as a health professional. I am so proud of her.

She brings the girls by for me to see them. Last time, she asked, "Am I a good mother, Miss Helen?" My answer was "Yes!" One day she came in and told me she had met a young man. I asked her about him, and I told her I needed to meet him. She said, "Are you serious, Miss Helen?" My reply to Lisa was "Yes, I am your other mother!" Lisa looked at me with tears in her eyes and said, "Miss Helen, you are my mother."

God expects us to walk the whole mile with those in need. Are these ladies and babies worth all the time and energy it takes to save their lives? The answer is resounding "Yes! Yes! Yes!"

# 2

## God's Got It

"But my God shall supply all your needs according to his riches in glory by Christ Jesus." Philippians 4:19 (KJV)

We give new baby clothes to the new moms when they come to us at the crisis pregnancy center. One month we were expecting well over 30 newborns and our supply of infant clothing was gone. The volunteers and I prayed and thanked God for providing for his precious little ones. The next day a local church called and asked what we needed. They collected 2,000 new 0-3 month outfits for the center. God is so good, and He always answers prayers. Many precious babies got clothes that winter because of the goodness and sharing spirit of God's people. Thank you God for your provision.

Another time we were trying to help over 300 children with Christmas gifts. Most of these families had lost their jobs due to the bad economy. Many churches contacted us wanting to know how they could help us during the holiday season. The churches responded with each child receiving at least three gifts, food, clothing, and the gift of the gospel! We told the parents that Jesus was the provider of the gifts for their children! These were definitely God Moments—times when God's love and power are most evident.

# 3

## *Wow, God!*

"Be not ye therefore like unto them: for your Father knoweth what things ye have need of, before ye ask him."
Matthew 6:8 (KJV)

The pregnancy centers rely on Christian people to provide for the financial expenses of the centers. We take no money from the government. Our mission is to share the love of Jesus with all. One November, times were tight, and I thanked God for providing for the needs of the centers. A soldier and his wife stopped by with diapers and clothes for the babies. Michael handed me an envelope as he left. I finished the night, and I opened the letter when I got home. The letter had a check for $10,000 in it. Thank you, Jesus. Two weeks later they returned, and again I was handed a letter. I thought it was a thank you note for a book I had given them. Again, I opened the letter, and once again it was a check for $10,000. Wow, God! That was such a God Thing. We serve an awesome God.

# 4

## God Has a Sweet Tooth

"O taste and see that the Lord is good: blessed is the man that trusteth in him." Psalm 34:8 (KJV)

Who doesn't have a sweet tooth? Well, did you know that God does? The pregnancy center has volunteers who come straight from work without stopping for food. They work hard, and there are no paid positions at the centers, only volunteers. Many times I try to keep snacks in the kitchen for the volunteers. We have one volunteer named Mim who is always looking for chocolate in the kitchen. I asked the Lord to bless us with some chocolate. A local store called and said they had some snacks for us. My husband went to pick up the donated snacks. He brought back $5,000 worth of chocolates. Mim was the happiest volunteer ever! We all decided that God has a sweet tooth and that He will give us our heart's desire—even chocolate. That definitely was such a God Thing.

# 5

## Love the Babies

"Take heed that ye despise not one of these little ones; for I say unto you that in heaven their angels do always behold the face of my Father." Matthew 18:10 (KJV)

I love how God provides for the centers. Adults, teenagers, and children all help with the centers. One night we were at the center and a beautiful red-headed little girl named Amy came in with her family. She had a shoebox in her hands. She walked over to me and handed me a box and said, "Love the babies." I opened the box, and there was $275 in cash. Her mother explained that Amy had a birthday and instead of presents she asked for money for the babies. She walked up to her birthday guests with the box and said, "Love the babies." I hugged her and thanked her. God said that a child would lead them. Amy may be little, but she has a God-shaped heart. That's a God Thing!

# 6

# Mama Cat

"And God said, Let the earth bring forth the living creature after his kind, cattle, and creeping thing." Genesis 1.24 (KJV)

One night at the center we had twenty clients in three hours. There were so many needs, and I was so tired. I had locked the door, turned out the lights, and started to leave when I saw a cat scratching on the front door. I went to the door and opened it. There was a pregnant cat, and she was hungry. I smiled as I thought about God sending a pregnant cat to the door of the crisis pregnancy center. I fed her, and in a couple of days she gave birth to four kittens. In the spirit of adoption, God provided good homes for the mama cat and her kittens. God has a way of reminding us that we are to care for His people and for His creatures.

# 7

## *Lemonade*

"Whosoever therefore shall humble himself as this little child, the same is the greatest in the kingdom of heaven." Matthew 18:4 (KJV)

Sammy is four years old. After listening about the center at his church, he decided to help the babies at the pregnancy center. He asked his mom to help him make some lemonade to sell. On a very hot summer day, he set up a lemonade stand and made a sign that said "For the babies". Sammy sat under his shade tree in his front yard and sold his lemonade for 50 cents a cup to help the babies. He came in to the center that Thursday with a $100 cash donation. You are never too young or too old to do the work of Jesus. Children helping children; now that's definitely a God Moment.

# 8

## Will You Adopt Me?

"To redeem them that were under the law, that we might receive the adoption of sons…" Galatians 4:5 (KJV)

Many of the young women who come to the pregnancy centers are very lonely and beaten down. I try to establish a relationship with these young mothers-to-be. We meet several times during the pregnancy. We do parenting classes, give baby clothes, and pray for them. One of the young women I was helping was telling me that she didn't have anybody. I asked her, "Who prays for you?" She said, "Nobody does." I told her that I would pray for her, and I did. As she left the room, she turned to me and said, "Miss Helen, will you adopt me?" Everyone needs to know that Jesus cares for him or her. He uses us to show that He cares!

# 9

## A Laundry Basket and Blinds

"Delight thyself also in the Lord, and he shall give thee the desires of thine heart." Psalm 37:4 (KJV)

I love the way God answers prayers, especially at the pregnancy ministry. We make layettes for new babies using laundry baskets. It is filled to the top with baby items for the newborns. We had an expectant mom that was coming in to get a layette for her twin girls. I checked in the back, and Mim said we were out of laundry baskets. We didn't even get an opportunity to pray for the basket. A lady came to our door and told us that God told her to bring us a laundry basket. We thanked her and God for the laundry basket. Then we set to work quickly preparing the layette for the twins. God had the answer on the way before we even knew we needed it!

Another time we had a client who had moved into a new apartment. We helped her with furniture and other needs. She had no curtains or blinds. I told her to pray that God would provide her with blinds. A lady came by the center with a $100 gift card. The gift card was for the blinds that were needed. I saw this young woman's faith grow all because of answered prayers for blinds.

God cares about everything in our lives, even laundry baskets and blinds.

# 10

## Prayer Answered – One Year Later

"I call heaven and earth to record this day against you, that
I have set before you life and death, blessing and cursing;
therefore choose life, that both thou and thy seed may live."
Deuteronomy 30:19 (KJV)

I have worked as a volunteer in crisis pregnancy centers for twenty-six years. I have learned that God answers prayers, sometimes right now and sometimes at a later date. I worked on Saturdays as a volunteer at a crisis pregnancy center. I met with clients each Saturday who were making life decisions. The center was on a road at the bottom of a hill with an abortion clinic at the top of the hill. There were even escorts to take the pregnant moms up the hill to kill their babies! Amy was a college student who would come to help me on Saturdays. We decided to pray that the abortion clinic would close. Our prayer included that the abortionists would come to know Jesus. If they didn't, we prayed that the women seeking abortions would not keep their appointments and that the abortion clinic would lose money. Amy and I were faithful and prayed every Saturday outside the abortion clinic.

Our prayers were answered one year later. We came to the pregnancy center, and the abortion clinic was closed. We asked, "What happened?" We were told that the abortion clients were not keeping their appointments and that the abortion clinic had gone bankrupt. Praise God! Never give up when you are praying. Answered prayers are truly God Moments.

# 11

## *Superglue*

"What shall we then say to those things? If God is for us, who can be against us?" Romans 8:31 (KJV)

We at the crisis pregnancy center try to get the word out that we are here to help pregnant women who are in crisis. One of the ways we do that is by securing billboards. We are a non-profit, so we usually have to pay $300 for one month of advertising. The lady we deal with said that she usually left the billboards up for one month. She said that the billboard glue usually lasted only thirty days. We had an advertisement for life put up on one of their billboards, and God superglued the billboard. The billboard stayed up for more than just thirty; it stayed up for nine months. God super-glued it! Nothing is impossible with God!

# 12

## Guardian Angel on Duty

"Be not forgetful, to entertain strangers; for thereby some
have entertained angels unawares." Hebrews 13:2 (KJV)

The pregnancy ministry is on the rough side of town and the building
that we now have used to be an abortion clinic. There are pimps,
prostitutes, alcoholics, homeless, and drug addicts right outside our
door. The volunteers all keep an eye on each other as we come and
go for safety reasons. One night, we all headed for our cars. I got in
mine, and the car wouldn't crank. All the volunteers were gone. All
around me were the street people and lots of sin activities. I tried
to call my husband and couldn't get him. At that moment, a young
man appeared beside my car. I let down my window and asked if
I could help. He said, "Helen, I will take care of you until your
husband gets here. I take care of the pregnancy center when you are
not here. Go ahead and call your husband. You are safe." We talked,
and my husband Ed finally drove up. I turned to thank the young
man for staying with me. He was gone. I looked around. I asked Ed
if he had seen the young man. He said he didn't see anybody. Was
this a guardian angel that the Lord sent to protect me? Thank you,
Jesus, for watching over me.

# 13

## Pastor with Hidden Secret

"Confess your faults one to another, and pray for one another, that ye may be healed. The effectual fervent prayer of a righteous man availeth much." James 5:26 (KJV)

I speak in many churches each year for the life ministries. Recently, I spoke at a women's conference. I spoke about life and the life-long effects of abortion. I could tell the Lord was dealing with those who had past abortions. Afterwards, a pastor came up and asked if he could meet with me the following week. This pastor came to the center the following week. We talked and then he shared his story. He wept as he shared that he had gotten three girls pregnant before he accepted Jesus. He talked the young women into aborting their babies and paid for the abortions. Later on, he accepted Jesus, and God called him into the ministry. He is married now, and they desire children. They have prayed eight years for a child! He said he wondered if this was God's punishment for the abortions. I told him he must tell his story so that others would choose life. Abortion affects more that the women; it impacts the fathers and the entire family. This pastor is in healing mode. Now for the rest of this story-- I went to speak at another event, and the pastor was there. He came up to me smiling and said, "Miss Helen, here is a picture of my precious daughter. She was born Monday and weighed five pounds. I named her Grace. God is so good." Please pray for those that have been affected by abortion. Abortion is a killer and a destroyer led by the devil himself. Praise God for His Amazing Grace.

# 14

## Joshua Caleb

"I will praise thee; for I am fearfully and wonderfully made; marvelous are thy works; and my soul knoweth right well." Psalm 139:14 (KJV)

The pregnancy ministry helps meet the needs of all kinds of clients. I had a young eighteen-year-old girl who was from a different religion call to ask about making a choice for her baby. She was ten weeks pregnant and undecided about what to do with her baby. The father of the baby was a soldier who was deployed. She was afraid of her parents who would have her returned to her country because she had brought shame on her family. I talked to her and asked if she would like a free ultrasound. We made an appointment for her to return for the ultrasound. Sarah (not her real name) returned, and you could see a beautiful baby boy bouncing around in the womb. In one of the ultrasound pictures he placed his hands to his chin in prayer mode. I told her that he was praying to my Jesus. She took the ultrasound pictures and was going to make copies to send to the father of the baby. She chose life that day for her precious son.

Joe and Sarah made plans to marry. She knew she had to get away from her family. She was pregnant out of wedlock, and in her culture this was a dishonor to her family. Plans were made to get her to a safe place. The day before Mother's Day, someone told Sarah's mother that she was pregnant. Her mother put her in the car against her will and took her to the abortion clinic. That precious little boy died that day.

I cried for three days over the death of this child. I asked God to show us what to do to give value to this precious little boy. I named him Joshua Caleb. God led us to open a pregnancy center in a building right across from the abortion clinic where little Joshua lost his life. We are fighting the battle for life right in the face of the enemy. I feel like we are David, and the abortion clinic is Goliath. We know what happened to Goliath. We pray for the closing of this abortion clinic and have prayed that God will give us the building for one dollar. The battle is intense and we will continue to fight for all the other Joshua Calebs to live.

# 15

## *He is still God.*

"For we walk by faith, not by sight." 2 Corinthians 5:7
(KJV)

This adventure begins the day I met Joshua's mom. On that particular day, I had a doctor's appointment that turned into three months of events. They found a five-inch mass on my thyroid. My precious daughter called me and said that God had revealed to her that the enemy was trying to steal my voice since I speak for the babies who cannot speak for themselves. They scheduled the surgery and did a biopsy. All looked well. I went in for surgery on June 25th, and again they did a biopsy. This time they found thyroid cancer, and a second surgery was scheduled for two weeks later. I got an infection, and it was tough. Since I no longer have a thyroid, I now need thyroid medication. If you have thyroid cancer, you go through a procedure which uses radioactive iodine. During the three weeks before this procedure you cannot take thyroid medicine, and it makes you very weak.

Listen to what this procedure required you to do. You have to receive a small portion of radioactive iodine and do two full body scans. Then according to the results, you are given more radioactive iodine. While you are taking this iodine, you are in isolation and cannot be around pregnant women and children for five days. I was sitting at home in isolation and praying that all of the cancer cells would be killed.

I appreciated all the prayers and the cards. I have always said that if everything was taken from me that Jesus would be enough. I could NOT do the centers, teach my Sunday school class, teach my kindergarten class, follow through on my speaking engagements, be near my family as we had two grandbabies on the way, or be near my sweet, precious husband. To top it off, my voice was growly. The insurmountable bills started coming in from all the surgeries. I felt like Job especially when I had a friend who came by and prayed that I would know what sin in my life was causing this, and it must be the people that I was around that God had allowed this to happen in my life. Just what I needed to hear! Is Jesus enough when all looks dark? The answer is YES, YES, YES! He is still God, and He is in control. It is not what I do for Jesus that makes Him love me; He just loves me. But I am so glad that He wants to use me.

I asked God that His name would be glorified during this adventure. My doctor was Hindu, and I got an opportunity to witness to him twice and give him my book *God Loves You Better Than Mac and Cheese*. The two nurses at the office asked for prayer. While I was sitting in the hospital room recovering from the surgery, a young woman called and asked how much an abortion was. We talked, and she chose life. The list goes on. I did not choose that valley, but Praise God He allowed it. He saw me through it.

# 16

## Jesus and the Earthquake

"For the kingdom of God is not in word, but in power." 1 Corinthians 4:20 (KJV)

Yvonne came to the crisis center pregnancy, scared, alone, and with a language barrier. She was from Haiti and left during the big earthquake. Her mother, father, sister, and brothers were killed. Her boyfriend was missing, and she assumed he was dead. Yvonne was in a strange land, pregnant, and alone. I counseled Yvonne about Jesus and His love. She accepted Jesus, and we helped her with baby items. She had a beautiful baby boy named Bray. Yvonne loved him and was a good mother. A couple of months later Yvonne got word that her boyfriend was alive and that he was on his way to America. Her prayer had been answered. Yvonne and Sam asked to be married at the center. It was such a sweet wedding. My husband Ed did the ceremony. Yvonne and Sam stood before Ed with Bray in his stroller between them. During the ceremony, Bray put his hands up taking his Mom and Dad's hands. God is so good! That was such a God Thing. Sam found a job out-of-state, and so they prepared to leave. Yvonne's request was that she wanted to be baptized. Ed baptized her at our church. Isn't it awesome how God used an earthquake to help Yvonne come to know Jesus? By the way, her husband also got saved, and Bray has a Christian Mom and Dad. God is so good!

# 17

## Joshua Caleb's Letter

"Lo, children are a heritage of the Lord and the fruit of the
womb is his reward." Psalm 127:3 (KJV)

Is God enough when all is taken? Remember this story of Joshua
Caleb? Well here is Joshua's side of the story:

Hi! Today my Mommy came to the Agape Center. She was not
sure if she was going to keep me. Miss Helen talked to her and told
her that I was a precious baby. Mom even held a little model of a
twelve-week-old in her hand as she was counseled. My Mommy is
not a Christian, but my Daddy is. He is serving our country. Miss
Helen even told my Mom that she could get a free ultrasound.
Mom came in a week later. I wanted to show her that I was alive; I
showed off during the ultrasound. I waved my hands and bounced
around. I even put my prayer hands under my chin so she could see
me. My Mom was so excited. She kept showing everyone my head
and fingers and my tummy. Mom found out that I was a boy. She
took the pictures of the ultrasound, and she was going to Walmart
to make enlargements to send to my Dad. She was so happy.

You see, she chose me, and that meant that she would never see
her family again. In Mom's religion, she had done a horrible thing by
being pregnant out-of-wedlock. Mom made plans to leave her home
and go live with a friend until Daddy could get back. Everything was
in order. I was growing and moving around. I could feel Mommy
close to me. Mom was going to keep me. Then something terrible
happened today.

My grandmother found out that Mom was pregnant, and she took her to this terrible place called an abortion clinic. I died on May 10th. I am with Jesus. That is good, but I wanted to live the life that God had for me on earth. My Mommy is sad, and she cries a lot. Daddy is sad; he feels guilty because he could not protect me. Please pray for my Mommy and Daddy. By the way, Miss Helen named me Joshua Caleb. Miss Helen cried for me for three days. Do you realize how many other babies died the same day I did? Will you please let my short life make a difference for other babies?

P.S. Daddy and Mommy got married; they miss me a lot. Please pray for them!

# 18

## Faith Returns

"For I know the thoughts that I think toward you, saith
the Lord, thought of peace, and not of evil, to give you an
expected end." Jeremiah 29:11 (KJV)

I have been involved in life ministries for twenty-six years. I tell
people that I have seen 14,000 babies born that could have died to
abortion. I call these children my "godchildren." Not too long ago,
a young woman came into the center. She asked me if I remembered
her. She said, "I am the one who called for an abortion six years ago.
I was about to be evicted from my home the next day. I had no food,
no hope, and I was pregnant. You helped me to see that I was carrying
a precious baby. You paid my rent, and you gave me food. You helped
me through the pregnancy and provided love and support during
my difficult time. I was challenged by you to go back to school and
to get a degree. I was reminded that God had someone special for
me to marry. You told to be patient, and wait on the Lord was your
counsel." I hugged her, and she said, "I want you to meet someone.
This is Faith, she is six years old." Faith was standing behind her
mother. Faith came out, and she was beautiful. Her mother told me
that she was a witness to everybody about God's love. She also helped
to lead worship at church. Sue has gone back to school and now was
a nurse. She was not married yet but was waiting on the Lord to
send her a husband. God gave me a glimpse of one of the lives that
have been touched by our life ministry. We do not always get to see
what God does in the lives of our clients. We may never know until
we reach Heaven. God does encourage us as we walk this life's path.

# 19

## A Rainbow and a New Beginning

"For it is God which worketh in you both to will and to do of his good pleasure." Philippians 2:13 (KJV)

Rainbows are special to me. It seems that when there are major events going on in my life, God always sends me a rainbow. One night at the pregnancy ministry I had a client named Amy who had been in an abusive relationship. She was feeling worthless, abused, and suicidal. She was eight months pregnant. I counseled her that God loves her and that He desires to be her Lord and Savior. She wept as she asked Jesus into her life. As she accepted Jesus, Amy became a new creation in Christ. You could see hope returning. I prayed with her, and we helped her with clothes and diapers. I walked her to the door. We looked at the sky and saw a beautiful full rainbow. There had been no rain. I believe God sent this rainbow sign to Amy as a promise of His Love.

# 20

## *Haley's Gift*

"Therefore, whoever humbles himself like this child is the
greatest in the Kingdom of heaven."
Matthew 18:4 (KJV)

I taught Kindergarten for forty years. One of my favorite students
was Haley. Haley was a blessing. She had a tough beginning. Her
mom was killed when Haley was two years old and her brother was
under a year old. Now they are being raised by godly grandparents.
One day Haley gave me a beautiful apple purse. I told her thank you,
and she told me that it had been her mom's. That was such a God
Thing. At the end of the school year, Haley brought me a beautiful
framed picture of Jesus holding a little girl's hand. She told me to
put it at the pregnancy center. Later the granddaddy told me that
the picture had belonged to Haley's mom when she was a little girl.
Haley had kept it in her room after her mom died. Wow! What a gift
of love. Haley shared her love with all around her. What the devil
meant for evil, God used for His Glory.

# 21

## Lebron – The Homeless Man

"God is our refuge and strength, a very present help in trouble." Psalm 46:1 (KJV)

The crisis pregnancy center is not on the sunny side of town. We get many people from many walks of life. One night a big, burly man came in. He said he was hungry and tired. He had not had a bath in fifteen days. His home was under the bridge and an abandoned building. He cried as he told how he had come to the city to find a job. Hard times were upon him. He wept as he asked if we could help. We got him some food, and I asked one of the male volunteers to carry him to a local motel for the night. When Lebron came in, he smelled rough. Before he left, he hugged me and thanked us for the help. It was funny; I couldn't smell him at all. He had the aroma of Christ. Brian took him to the motel where he got a wonderful shower, food to eat, and a bed to sleep in, compliments of Jesus. I have not seen Lebron since that night. I often wonder if he was an angel sent by God to test us. I think of him often and lift him up in prayer. Look around; there are individuals who need the touch of Christ.

# 22

## *Not Another Child*

"Trust in the Lord with all your heart and lean not on your own understanding." Proverbs 3:5 (KJV)

The crisis pregnancy center helps women married and unmarried. We had a woman call who had a three-year-old, a two-year-old, and a nine-month-old girl. She was expecting her fourth child in a month. She was married, and finances were limited. She asked for an abortion, and we offered her a free ultrasound. Both her and her husband showed up and went into the ultrasound room. Soon, I heard laughter, and I stuck my head in. The baby was a boy. They realized at that moment that this child would not be aborted. We helped her with clothes, diapers, food, and prayer. They would have missed a blessing if they had chosen abortion. We need to look at every situation through God's eyes instead of human eyes. God's timing is always best. Trust Him; you will be blessed instead of stressed.

# **23**

## *$1,606.07*

"Cast thy bread upon the waters; for thou shalt find it after many days." Ecclesiastes 11:1 (KJV)

The pregnancy ministries run entirely on donations from the Christian community. January is always a skinny financial month. We needed a certain amount to pay our bills for the month. I thanked God for the $1,606.07 that He would send to meet the need. It was the last day of January. A young soldier and his family came in and handed me a check. I thanked him and opened the check, and the amount was $1,606.07. This was the exact amount needed for January. God is an on-time God.

# 24

## *Sarah*

"My substance was not hid from thee, when I was made in secret, and curiously wrought in the lowest parts of the earth." Psalm 139:15 (KJV)

One of the precious women who came to the pregnancy center was a young teacher. She was pregnant by a man who had gotten nine women pregnant and had them abort their children. Now he was trying to get Sarah to abort her child. She thought about it and even went to the abortion clinic. She couldn't do it. All of Sarah's family was encouraging her to abort her child. We helped her, counseled her, and gave her an ultrasound. She struggled with her decision. Many times during the pregnancy she would ask me, "How will I know if I made the right choice?" She had a beautiful seven-pound baby boy and named him Samuel. She came back to the center carrying her precious son. She looked at me and said, "Miss Helen, I made the right decision. I love my son, and he is a blessing. God will help me raise my son." The God Moment was the minute she looked into the eyes of her precious son.

# 25

## Becky and Sue

"My little children, let us not love in word, neither in tongue, but in deed and truth." 1 John 3:18 (KJV)

Miss Becky came to the pregnancy center one night. She was fifty-five years old. She cried as she told her story. When she was sixteen years old, she got pregnant. She planned to abort her baby but changed her mind. She worked hard providing for her son. When her son was six years old, he and his older cousin found a gun. The gun went off, and Miss Becky's son died. She was so sad.

The young man who pulled the trigger continued to follow a life of drugs and got in trouble with the law. This young man met a young woman in the drug scene. This woman got pregnant; she had no prenatal care. A beautiful four-pound baby girl was born. She was named Sue. Neither of Sue's parents wanted her. She was left at the hospital. Little Sue had drug withdrawal, and she fought to live. No family members wanted to take her. Sue's parents were sent to jail for drug charges. Miss Becky's kind heart reached out to little, abandoned Sue. She and her husband adopted Sue. Do you realize that Sue is the daughter of the man who killed Miss Becky's son? We prayed for peace and for Sue to be used mightily for the Savior. Again, I say what the devil meant for evil, God used for good. Thank you, God, that there are no throwaways in your creation.

# 26

## *God is Good*

"What shall we then say to these things? If God be for us,
who can be against us?" Romans 8:31 (KJV)

Jennifer came in one night to the center. She came to ask for food.
Jennifer asked me to please pray for a job for her. She was going
to be evicted from her home the next day at 12 noon. She and her
son would be on the streets. There was no family support. We had
prayer that God would send the $340 for her rent and that Jennifer
would get a job. A lady heard about Jennifer's need and gave $340
for her rent. She was also called in to start a new job the next day;
God had answered Jennifer's prayers within two hours. She texted
me with these words: "Miss Helen, God is soooo good. Thank you
for the prayers."

# 27

## Kel and the Plane

"And we know that all things work together for good to them that love God, to them who are called according to His purpose." Romans 8:28 (KJV)

I have taught forty years in Kindergarten. This past year, I went on an airplane trip to Texas to speak at a life banquet. I had never been on a plane in my entire life. I told my kindergarten students that I was going on a plane trip. I had been telling my students that we should always share Jesus no matter where we are. Kel looked at me and said, "Mrs. Rogers, ask everybody you see on the plane if they know Jesus, and then if the plane crashes, everybody on the plane will go to Heaven." It is simple, but what a beautiful way of looking at life. God tells us to have the faith of the child. Now that's love – God's love!

# 28

## *Tell It*

"Lo children are a heritage of the Lord and the fruit of the
womb is his reward." Psalm 127:3 (KJV)

In the previous story, I told about my kindergarten class and how we
had been learning that walking with Jesus means telling everyone
we meet about Him. I told my class I had a doctor's appointment.
I was not sure of this doctor's faith. Haly looked at me and said,
"Mrs. Rogers, ask your doctor if she knows Jesus. If she doesn't, tell
her about God's love." It was simple but profound. By the way, my
doctor is a Christian. I asked my Korean doctor. She smiled and said,
"Yes, Jesus is my Lord and Savior." I reported back to Haly the next
day. She smiled and said, "You did good, Mrs. Rogers!" Now that
was such a God Thing.

# 29

## Big Boy – Not Fun

"As newborn babes, desire the sincere milk of the word,
that ye may grow thereby." 1 Peter 2:2 (KJV)

Cole is my four-year-old grandson. When he was two years old, his
mom was trying to break him from the bottle. He had been three
days without a bottle. I came to visit, and my daughter was bragging
on Cole and his three days of success. I told him I was proud of him
for giving up his bottle. I said, "Cole, I would like to bring you a
surprise for giving up your bottle. Do you want me to bring you a
tractor?" A side note – Cole loves tractors. Cole said, "No tractor."
I said, "If you don't want a tractor, what do you want?" He looked
at me, and with tears in his eyes he said, "I want my bottle back!"
So many times we are like Cole. God wants us to grow up, but we
want to hold on to the baby things. We lose blessings when we don't
grow up.

# 30

## *Put Tori Back*

"As newborn babes, desire the sincere milk of the word,
that ye may grow thereby." 1 Peter 2:2 (KJV)

Cole, my four-year-old grandson, got a new baby sister. He was so
excited while he was waiting for Tori. Tori came, and Cole's world
changed. He had been the center of attention, and now he felt as
though he were number two. One day Cole looked at his mom
and said, "Put Tori back in your tummy, Mommy!" Mom asked,
"Why?" Cole looked at his mom and said, "Tori takes too much
time." Growing up is so hard. In Jesus' eyes, we are number one.
We are all number one.

# 31

## Kids Say the Cutest Things

"Whosoever therefore shall humble himself as this little child, the same is the greatest in the kingdom of heaven." Matthew 18:4 (KJV)

Meet some of my kindergarten children:

Haly came into class and announced she had a wiggle worm. She meant to say ringworm.

Kel is a child who loves Jesus and wants everybody to know Him. We watched "Charlie Brown and the Great Pumpkin". Kel noticed that Lucy would always move the football when Charlie Brown tried to kick it. He raised his hand and said, "Mrs. Rogers, that Lucy girl needs Jesus. She is mean to Charlie Brown."

Children are precious gifts from God. Thank you, Jesus.

# 32

## God Owns a Turkey Farm

"Cast they bread upon the waters; for thou shall find it after many days." Ecclesiastes 11:1 (KJV)

I was at the pregnancy center, and a lady came be with a frozen turkey. I already had a turkey for my family for Thanksgiving. Sandy, one of my volunteers came in. She is in charge of a local food pantry. She shared with me that she was trying to get a Thanksgiving meal for a needy family. Sandy had some canned food but needed a meat for them. I told her a lady just delivered a turkey, and she could have it for the family. She smiled and said, "I know God owns the cattle on a thousand hills; I didn't realize He owned turkey farms, too." God always provides when we walk in faith. Why do we ever doubt Him?

# 33

## Sweet Jesus

"Oh taste and see that the Lord is good..." Psalm 34:8
(KJV)

When I was born, I was named after my grandmother. I was the first born granddaughter, and she spoiled me. She sewed me beautiful dresses. My favorite treat was hot, homemade biscuits and chocolate syrup. I would spend the night with Grandma and Grandpa. Nothing was finer than sleeping in that big, soft bed between them.

Since I was her favorite grandchild (my observation), Grandma always saved me pieces of chocolate candy. One day I came to visit and looked in the top dresser drawer for my candy treat. I found a new candy in little squares. I ate the whole pack. Later on, I noticed that I had to go to the outhouse a lot. I found out that the chocolate candy was Ex-lax. So many times I see Christians who look like they have had a dose of Ex-lax instead of a sweet taste of Jesus. If Jesus is in our hearts, there should be smiles on our faces and joy in our hearts. The Bible reminds us to taste and see that the Lord is good.

# 34

## *The Dandelion*

"Every good gift and every perfect gift is from above, and cometh down from the Father of lights." James 1:17 (KJV)

My daughter had a son named Adam. He was my first grandson. Adam died after a few hours on earth. A lady sent Marsha a beautiful poem about a dandelion. Even though a dandelion is a weed, in the hands of a child it is a flower of love. Four years later, God gave us another grandson named Cole. I had prayed that God would give me a grandson to catch frogs, play in the mud, climb forts, and pee in my face when I changed his diaper. God blessed us with a very busy, handsome, little Cole who brings joy to us all.

On Adam's birthday, Cole, who was two years old, picked a handful of dandelions and gave them to his mom. She took the dandelion bouquet from his little hands, and a flood of memories of Adam and the dandelion poem sent a hug to her heart. God has a way of reminding us that He has not forgotten our pains and will give us new joys. Marsha will see Adam again, and her family will be complete. That's a promise from God. God divides our sorrows and doubles our joys.

# 35

## *Nutty Fall*

"If we confess our sins, he is faithful and just to forgive us our sins." 1 John 1:9 (KJV)

It was after Christmas, and I was going out to the front yard to take the manger scene down. As I was walking across the yard, I slipped on some acorns. I fell back and hit my head on the car. I busted my head, and it took fourteen stitches to sew it up. I had a very sore head for a couple of weeks. Sometimes in life it is not the huge stumbling blocks that get us; it is the small acorns. When I went to the emergency room, they could not believe that a small acorn could cause that much damage. A small problem can become a big one unless we take care of it. A small sin can become a big one if we do not take it to the Lord and ask for forgiveness.

# 36

## *Time For Jesus*

"Take heed that ye despise not one of these little ones..."
Matthew 18:10 (KJV)

I have shared that I was a kindergarten teacher for forty years. I tried to keep Jesus before them all day. One of the ways I shared Jesus was a clock that chimes a hymn on the hour. When the students heard the clock, they all stopped and said, "I love you, Jesus. Thank you, Jesus!" One day I had my principal in the room; he was evaluating my teaching. The students were in centers all over the room busy working. The clock chimed on the hour. All the students got quiet, and you could hear the words "I love you, Jesus" and "thank you, Jesus." As soon as they said it, they went back to work and play. The principal asked, "What happened?" I smiled and said it was a class secret. He was in awe. We are to praise Him, all infants, children, and adults. Because of the presence of the Lord in my class, there were very few discipline problems. Jesus is our plumb line (the standard for our lives). Now that was such a God Thing.

# 37

## *Tough Beginning*

"What shall we say to these things? If God be for us, who can be against us." Romans 8:31 (KJV)

I was born to my parents in 1950. Mom was only eighteen years old. She had a hard delivery and went into a coma after I was born. I was left in a crib in Mama's hospital room while she was in a coma. One day I had pooped all over myself. The nurse came in and started fussing at me. She said she was going to throw me away because I was in a mess. My mom woke up from her coma and said, "Give me my baby. Nobody's going to throw my baby away." I am glad that Mama loved me even in my mess. Mama's love is like God's love. Even in our mess, He loves us. Aren't you glad?

# 38

## *The Picture*

"Then spake Jesus again saying, I am the light of the
world…" John 8:12a (KJV)

I share Jesus with all who enter the doors of the pregnancy ministry.
One of the things I share is about a picture of Jesus. When I was
growing up, there was a painting of Jesus knocking on the door. You
cannot see the people inside. I asked Mom, "Where is the doorknob
so Jesus can come in?" I noticed it was missing. Mom said, "The
door can only be opened from the inside. Jesus can only go in where
He is invited." Jesus wants us to choose Him; He's a God of love. He
is not pushy. Today the Lord is knocking on your heart's door. Will
you open the door and let Jesus in? He loves you!

# 39

## Gorgeous

"Blessed are the pure in heart, for they shall see God."
Matthew 5:8 (KJV)

I have a wonderful grandson named Cole. He is a talker and started talking early in life. I was walking on the beach with Cole when he was two years old. He would pick up a shell and say "gorgeous shell." He picked up every shell he would see. Some of the shells were broken, some only pieces, but to my Cole, they were all "gorgeous."

We can learn from this child. God sees the beauty in us even when we are broken. God is our Creator, and He can use us for His service and glory even when we are broken.

# 40

## *The Dead Cat*

"In everything give thanks: for this is the will of God in
Christ Jesus concerning you." 1 Thessalonians 5:18 (KJV)

One of my favorite kindergarten memories was a student named
Ben. Ben brought in many interesting show-and-tell items each
day. His most interesting one was the day he brought in a dead cat
for show-and-tell. Ben walked in with a big bag, and I asked him
what was in the bag. He said, "Mrs. Rogers, I brought a dead cat
for show-and-tell." I smiled, thinking that Ben was teasing me and
that he had a stuffed animal in the bag. I told him to put the bag
on the back table.

The class started with ABCs and 123s and what is that smell?
I walked over to Ben's bag and looked inside, and there was a dead
cat in the bag. I asked God what I should do with Ben and the dead
cat. God said that I must speak life into this situation. I called all the
students over and told them that Ben had a special show-and-tell. We
did not take the cat out of the bag; I just let the students look into
the bag. All the students looked. Some said things like "that's gross,"
and "I'll give you my lunch money for the cat." The show-and-tell
time was finished. I put the dead cat on the patio for fresh air.

The day ended, and I asked the Lord, "What am I supposed to
do with this dead cat?" God said, "How did it get here?" I replied,
"The bus, Lord." He told me to send it home on the bus. I tied up
the bag and gave it to the bus driver and told her not to open the
bag. I reminded her that the bag had to get off with Ben. The bus
driver looked a little scared.

That night I got a call from Ben's mom. She apologized for the dead cat. I asked her if Ben got the cat home okay. She said that the cat was home now; it had been to choir practice and boy scouts with Ben. Dad and Ben had just buried the cat in the backyard. Ben's mom said that if I needed anything this year to please let her know. I told her I would send a list tomorrow of things needed for the classroom. My question to you is what do you do with the dead cats in your life? God says that every situation should be handled with the words of life.

# 41

## *Precious Memories*

"Lo, children are a heritage of the Lord: and the fruit of the womb is his reward." Psalm 127:3 (KJV)

I shared this story in my book, *God Loves You Better Than Mac and Cheese*. I have four precious granddaughters, and I have one precious grandson on earth. Eight years ago, God gave us a grandson for a little while. Here is the letter I read at his funeral. There may be someone that is reading this that is hurting from the loss of a child. Remember Jesus is our Hope; our only Hope.

Dear Adam,

We just want you to know we love you, and we already miss you. You came into our lives about eight months ago when your mom told us we were going to have a new grandchild. We were so excited. You see, Kassi, your big sister, asked Santa for a baby. That did not work, so she decided to ask God for a baby sister. In January we found out that God had answered Kassi's prayers. We started guessing if you were a boy or a girl.

We were so excited! Kassi and Heidi finally decided that a baby brother was okay. Marsha started going for appointments, keeping us updated on the progress of this new addition to our family. We prayed that your life would honor God.

Then one day in April, we got the terrible news that you, our precious grandson, had lots of health problems, and the doctors gave you a zero percent chance of living. I remember weeping and praying for you. You see the doctors thought you would die in the womb. But Adam, we know the Heavenly Father, and we prayed for your healing. And God did heal you, sweetheart, so you could stay with us for a little while. Kassi and Heidi's prayers consisted simply of "God, take care of baby Adam." Many people were praying for you.

I want you to know, Adam, that your mom and dad fought to give you life. The doctors wanted to abort you, but your mama and daddy said that God is the author of life and death. They trusted God with His plan for you. They did all that was humanly possible for you. Adam, we prayed for your healing, and God did heal you. Even now you are in the arms of Jesus; you are whole and in no pain.

Adam, you were perfect to us. You were so cute with tiny hands, reddish-blond hair, Kelvin's toes, and that cute little smile. Mama and Daddy named you Joshua Adam, which means Saved by the Lord and made in the image of God. You fought so hard to stay with us. I watched your little heart rate go up as your daddy and mama held you and talked to you. We all watched as your heart rate would go down again and then your sisters would sing "Jesus Loves Me" to you, and the rate would become steady again.

Adam, many people will not understand how we could love you so deeply since in their eyes you only lived for five hours. In our hearts, you lived eight months on this earth, and now you will be a part of our lives forever. Adam, you taught us about life and love. Little One, all babies should have what you had, a safe place to grow inside your mom, a loving family, and a big God. You have made this family stronger in love and have helped us to rededicate our lives fighting for other babies in the womb. Thanks, Adam; we love you!

I remember asking God one day, "Why did my little Adam die?" God said, "I have a plan for Adam's life just as I do for all my people." Whether you live one minute, for hours, or one hundred years, it should be all for God's Glory. Because we love Jesus, Adam, we simply will say we will see you soon.

Forever in our Hearts,
Love, your family
P.S. Five years later, God blessed us with a grandson named Cole. Now I have a grandson in Heaven and one to play with down here. God is so good!

# 42

## *Fellow Believer*

"For the kingdom of God is not in word, but in power." 1
Corinthians 4:20 (KJV)

I went to Methodist College in Fayetteville for my degree. Every day
at lunch, I would meet in the Oasis with ten friends. Most of these
friends were unsaved except one. Her name was Joyce. Joyce and I
served Jesus, and we were best friends. Joyce and I started praying for
the people in our group. Graduation came, and Joyce and I walked
to get our diplomas. Joyce was to be married the next week. She was
so excited. We hugged that graduation day, and I told her I would
see her at the wedding.

Wednesday of the following week, I received a call telling me
that Joyce had been killed in a car accident. She had been on her way
to get wedding details in order. I grieved over the death of my friend.
She would never get married, raise a family, and grow old. I also
rejoiced that she was saved and in Heaven. I wonder if the witness
she shared with that group of young people impacted them. I wrote
a letter to Joyce's parents telling them of her witness for Christ. We
must be ready for we do not know the time we will leave this earth.

# 43

## Answered Prayer

"In everything give thanks; for this is the will of God in
Christ Jesus concerning you." 1 Thessalonians 5:18 (KJV)

My husband and I accepted the call to the ministry twelve years into
our marriage. It was our first time leaving parents and our home. We
packed up our furniture and our kids and headed to Nashville, NC.
It was a hard move. We had left a vibrant church, a loving family,
and lot of friends. God placed us in the middle of fields, chickens,
and farms. I was so lonely.

We had a beautiful, elderly Christian lady who lived in an old
colonial home with beautiful gardens. She had children but didn't
get to see them much. I would go and visit, and we would have
Bible studies together. We enjoyed long walks through the garden
together. She had taught in the one-room schoolhouse and had been
a principal for fifty years. Miss Cole had taught the same Sunday
school class for fifty years. I loved Miss Cole.

One day as we were walking, I told her that I didn't know why
God had sent me here. I missed my family. She smiled and said, "You
are an answer to my prayer. I prayed you here; I needed a friend."
When she died, I was with her. She quietly walked into Heaven. I
look forward to seeing her again. It is wonderful to be someone's
answer to prayer. Today be obedient to God, and you may be an
answered prayer to someone in need.

# 44

## Divine Appointment

"Bear ye one another's burdens and so fulfill the law of Christ." Galatians 6:2 (KJV)

My son Tom had very high fevers when he was little. Many times we would end up at the hospital. This happened on one of those trips back to the hospital. I needed to be with my son at the hospital, but I also needed to be with the other four children at home. One night while I sat in the hospital rocking chair, I heard a child crying down the hall. Tom was asleep, and I put him in the crib and tiptoed down the hall. The crying was coming from the room at the end.

I peeked in, and there was a six-year-old girl and a seven-year-old boy. The girl was crying. I asked her if I could help her. She told me she had been in a car accident. Her mother, daddy, and older sister had died in the accident. It was just her and her brother. Relatives from Florida were coming to pick them up. I prayed for her, and every night I would go down and talk to her.

I left the hospital long enough to go home and get some fresh clothes. I was trying to think of something, I could share with Leslie. There on the shelf was my treasured music box that my friend brought me from Switzerland. I picked it up and took it back to the hospital. That night I took it to Leslie and told her that when she was lonely and afraid to listen to the music box. The music box would remind her of how much God loved her. Later on that night, I heard the music from the music box. I often think of her and pray for her. Sometimes God allows us to go through things because he has some Divine Appointments for us. Look for your God Moments.

# 45

## The Right Attitude

"Blessed are the pure in heart, for they shall see God."
Matthew 5:8 (KJV)

God has blessed me with some special children during my forty years of teaching. Germaine was one of these special children. He had swallowed Drano when he was two years old. It ate his throat up, and he had to be fed with liquids through a special tube. No other kindergarten teacher wanted Germaine in her class. I asked for him to be placed in my class. He had to wear a bib, and he drooled a lot. He made sounds, but they weren't audible. Germaine had the most beautiful smile and the greatest hug. Germaine was in a wheelchair, and the kids would fight over who would roll him around the school. The children all accepted Germaine and loved him. When Germaine couldn't come to school, I would take his school work to him. No matter what was going on with him, he was happy. I was blessed by this precious child. He made every day a good day. We should face every day as this little child. No matter what kind of situations we are going through, it is important to have the attitude of Christ.

# 46

## *Problem Solving*

"Rejoice in the Lord…" Psalm 33:1a (KJV)

Cole was twenty-two months old when his mama was expecting a new baby sister. His mom kept telling Cole that his new sister was in her tummy. Cole couldn't quite understand that concept. So one day Cole got the trashcan and went to his mom and said, "Throw up my baby sister, Mommy!" We all laughed. Cole was ready to see his sister, and he was doing some problem solving. Children are a blessing and add much joy to our lives.

# 47

## Bloom Where You Are Planted

"For it is God which worketh in you both to will and to do of his good pleasure." Philippians 2:13 (KJV)

One of the centers where I volunteer is on the rough side of town. I planted flowers one spring, and they were beautiful. They really brightened up the building and the neighborhood. The next spring, I was walking up on the brick steps beside the garden, and there was a beautiful petunia. A small seed had gotten in some dirt in the hole in the brick. There it had bloomed. I couldn't help but thank God for the beauty of His creation and how we are not always planted in a beautiful garden. Sometimes we are planted in difficult places. We should all be like this flower blooming where God plants us.

# 48

## *Psalm 139*

"If a Thought Were a Grain of Sand"
Inspired by Psalm 139

If a thought were a grain of sand,
My thoughts toward you I could hold in my hand,
But your thoughts towards me, O LORD,
Are more than all the sand by the shore.
When I was formed in the depths of the earth,
Even before the day of my birth,
You knew every day that I was to be
And you made a way for me.
You hem me in behind and before,
And you make my way secure.
You watch me through the darkest of nights,
And wake me with the morning light.
When I close my eyes in death,
When I breathe my very last breath,
I will walk on the golden shore
To be with You forever and ever more.
If a thought were a grain of sand,
My thoughts toward you I could hold in my hand,
But your thoughts toward me, O LORD,
Are more than all the sand by the shore.

~ Marilyn Dawn Rogers
This poem was written by my daughter after the death of my
mother (her grandmother).

# 49

## *Zucchini*

"A merry heart doeth good like a medicine." Proverbs 17:22a (KJV)

This is one of my favorite stories from my book called, *God Loves You Better Than Mac and Cheese.*

I have been teaching kindergarten for forty years. One of my favorite stories is about two precious students who made my life very interesting. Their names were Ben and Wilson. I was working at a school in Rocky Mount, North Carolina. My husband was a pastor in a small church, and the money I made was our main source of income. This particular year the county school system had a new evaluation system for teachers. The teacher would have a scheduled day, and four evaluators would come into your room to observe you. It was my turn the next day for the evaluations.

Ben and Wilson were very energetic boys and were always into everything. My prayer for the next day was "Dear Lord, please keep Ben and Wilson home tomorrow. You don't have to make them sick; just please let them miss the bus." Guess who the first two students were to come in the next day? You guessed it, Ben and Wilson. My prayer changed to "Dear Lord, please let me keep my job." The day started, and the evaluators came in with their pads and stern looks.

Our class was studying "z" words. I asked the class to give me some "z" words, and they responded with words like zipper, zoo, zebra, and zoom. I asked if anyone else knew a "z" word, and Wilson raised his hand. I prayed for a good answer. His answer was "zucchini." I stopped, gulped, and thought "I don't know how to spell zucchini." The Lord told me to send Wilson to the library with a note. Let him find the word in the dictionary and come back and write it on the board. The librarian would help him. Wilson left the class and came back bouncing into the room. He wrote the word on the board. He was so proud of himself. (I knew it was right because the librarian wrote me a note.)

I asked Wilson, "What is a zucchini, Wilson?" He looked at me and answered, "You didn't tell me to find out what it was, Mrs. Rogers. You only told me to write it on the board." I asked the class if they knew the meaning of zucchini. Ben raised both his hands, and I knew the evaluators had seen since he was the only one with his hands up. I looked at Ben, prayed, and asked, "Ben, what is zucchini?" He stood up and put his hands on his hips and said, "Mrs. Rogers, zucchini, that's what women wear on the beach." Needless to say, the evaluators and I had a good chuckle over that answer. By the way, I got a great review that day. Oh, what I would have missed if God had answered my prayer to keep these two boys home.

# 50

## The Refrigerator and a Promise

"Because he hath set his love upon me, therefore will I deliver him; I will set him on high." Psalm 91:14

My dad was raised in a home with a godly mother and an alcoholic father. They are both deceased now. Daddy saw all the bad things that happened when alcohol is your god. My daddy said he promised God that strong drink would never be on his lips or in his home. He kept his promise. My dad was a strong, godly man who lived Jesus. One day our refrigerator broke, and an uncle let us borrow his refrigerator. My uncle came to visit and wanted to put his beer in the refrigerator. Daddy said, "No beer in the refrigerator, and if that is a problem you can take your beer and the refrigerator with you." My uncle left with the beer in the car, and the refrigerator stayed with us. My daddy followed the way of Jesus. He set the example for his children.

# 51

## Books Travel

"A word fitly spoken is like apples of gold in pictures of silver." Proverbs 25:11 (KJV)

I had prayed that the first book I wrote called *God Loves You Better Than Mac and Cheese* would travel across the United States and to other countries. There was a singing family that came to our town. I gave the mom one of my books. She took many books to pass out as she and her family traveled to Mexico, Canada, and the United States. God is an awesome God, and He has answered my prayers about using this book in ministering to others.

# 52

## *God Got Her Again*

"Ye are of God, little children, and have overcome them because greater is he that is in you, than he is in the world."
1 John 4:4 (KJV)

I have just retired from forty years of teaching kindergarten. The first thirty-five years I worked in public schools and the last five years in Christian schools. When we would have praise and worship time in the morning, the students would sing "I Can Only Imagine." The Holy Spirit was so strong when the children praised God. I would cry and raise my hands in praise. I heard Kel say, "Look, God's got Mrs. Rogers again; she is crying." God said that children would ordain praise.

# 53

## Willie's Turkey

"Delight thyself also in the Lord; and he shall give thee the desires of thine heart." Psalm 37:4 (KJV)

The pregnancy center helps many people. One of my favorite people is Willie. He is an elderly, diabetic man. He rides the bus to the pregnancy center. Willie comes in and says, "My mom and me are diabetics. We used all our money on medicine, and we are hungry. Do you have any food?" I always give him a bag of food. One day he came in and asked if we had a turkey. I told him we didn't, but I gave him some money to buy a turkey. He walked away smiling and singing. His last words as he left the center were "Bless you, Madame."

# 54

## From Death to Life

"For His anger endureth but a moment; in His favor is life: weeping may endure for a night, but joy cometh in the morning." Psalm 30:5 (KJV)

This is another one of my favorites from my book called, *God Loves You Better Than Mac and Cheese.*

My husband and I have been involved in starting crisis pregnancy centers in several counties in North Carolina. Ed is a pastor, and we felt the call to come to Fayetteville, North Carolina. We started the Agape Pregnancy Support Services in a house on Cedar Creek Road. After we had been there for two years, something happened to change our location. Fayetteville was the home of an abortion clinic that had been there for twenty-seven years. Many thousands of babies died in that clinic. Many Christians in the community would drive by the clinic and pray that the doors would close. God did answer their prayers, and the doors of the clinic closed.

The building was abandoned, and the homeless would sneak into the building at night. It was a horrible place.

One night I was restless, so I decided to read. My daughter had given me a book called *The Dream Giver* by Dr. Bruce Wilkerson. In the book the author talks about getting out of our comfort zone and walking by faith. The next morning God asked me to get out of my comfort zone and to go purchase the old abortion building. I told God I didn't want that building. I asked if He didn't have a new building we could have. I said, "Lord, this is a place of death." God said, "I have a special plan for this place. I am going to take back what Satan has used for evil and redeem it. I will bring life from this place, and it will bring glory and honor to me." I called the number on the building and asked the price. The price was $120,000. I reminded God that I was a kindergarten teacher, and I had only a few dollars until payday. I knew that God would have to provide the money. Ed and I went to the old building; it was a horrible mess. It was trashed with drug needles, beer, wine, and liquor bottles, rags, condoms, and human feces where the homeless had stayed.

The windows were boarded up, and it was very dark. We walked into the building carrying flashlights. You could fell the demonic powers in the place. We walked through the building shining the light into each room. Each room had a plan, and God revealed what it would be used for. At the back of the building, there were two procedure rooms with Formica walls and drainage in the floor. One procedure room had equipment left with blood on it and blood on the Formica walls. I stood at the door feeling as if I were going to throw up. God said, "You have to go into the room. You must feel what I feel." As I walked into the room, I could feel the pain and the sorrow. I heard babies crying because they didn't get to live the life that God had planned for them. They were also crying because they missed their moms. I heard the moms crying because they had killed their children. The third voice I heard in that room was my Lord and Savior weeping for all that was lost. My answer was to His call of obedience was "Yes!" He reminded me it would be hard and that the cost would be great. The answer was still "Yes!"

One month later, my mom died. God revealed that these two procedure rooms would be an ultrasound room and the other a chapel. The chapel would be a place for women to come and find forgiveness for their abortions. It would be a place to come out of the darkness into the light of Jesus. A man in our church did purchase the building, and we make payments each month. We started working on the building. We anointed every room in the building. We prayed, painted, and cleaned all for the glory of Jesus.

The first room to get the boards off of the windows was the chapel. As the boards came down, the light of Jesus flooded the chapel and the building. You could feel that Jesus had reclaimed what the enemy had for a season. I told my husband, "Look, Honey, there goes the devil with his packed bags, and he will not be coming back to this place."

The Agape Pregnancy Support Services is on the tough side of town. We have prostitutes, drug addicts, pimps, and the homeless walking the streets in front of the building. I had a dear Christian lady ask me if I knew what side of town the center was in. I smiled and said, "Yes, I do. I am exactly where Jesus would be." We know that God has placed us at this place. We are able to minister to the people of the street and our clients. I see God taking people from death to life eternally just as He did with this old abortion clinic. God is the Author of Life, both physical and eternal.

# 55

## *Real Treasure*

"For God so loved the world, that he gave his only begotten son, that whosoever believeth in him should not perish, but have everlasting life." John 3:16

The Agape Pregnancy Service is in a building that was an abortion clinic for twenty-seven years. The building was full of demons. There was even a safe in one of the rooms. This is where they put the blood money from the abortions. We figured that they killed 100,000+ babies in this place. I decided to put the real treasure in the safe. I put a Bible and the plan of salvation. If anyone breaks into the center's safe, they will find the true treasure. The true treasure is Jesus!

# 56

## The Eyes of a Child

"Blessed are the pure in heart, for they shall see God."
Matthew 5:8 (KJV)

We have many volunteers who help us at the pregnancy ministry. Sometimes the volunteers bring their children with them. Nicole brings Joey, her three-year-old with her. He is full of life. Many times when he comes to the center, he sees me ministering to the prostitutes on the street outside of our building. They sometimes will sit on the bench in our prayer garden. One day Joey came running into the center and said, "Miss Helen, Miss Helen, there is a girl sitting on our bench. She needs food, and she needs Jesus." You see, the girl he is talking about is a fifty-five-year-old prostitute. I told him I was getting some food together. He ran off to play in the playroom, and I went outside to the woman. I gave her some food and tried to talk to her about Jesus again. She walked away again without Jesus.

A little later, Joey came running into the counseling room and said, "Miss Helen, did you give the girl some food and tell her about Jesus?" I told him that I did and that we need to keep praying for the girl on the bench. He said good and that he would pray for her. Joey ran back to his world of play. You see, Joey has the eyes of Christ. He did not see the woman's sins; he saw a girl hungry and one who needed Jesus. Why can't we be more like Joey with the people we meet in the world? God tells us not to judge but to see each person the way that God sees them.

# 57

## *Uncle Truby*

"Bear ye one another's burdens, and so fulfil the law of Christ." Galatians 6:2 (KJV)

My daddy was a farmer, and on Saturdays he worked at a little grocery store in Lillington. Mr. Truby was a kind man, so we called him Uncle Truby. He and his wife didn't have any children, so they adopted us three girls. I would walk from the local high school after basketball practice to the store and wait for Daddy. Uncle Truby would give me a drink and a snack. Sometimes Daddy was late, and Uncle Truby would take me home. Later on, I figured out that he hired Daddy for Saturdays not because he needed him but to help our family during tough times. There are many people around us who make our lives better. God tells us to minister as we go. We should make a difference in all we meet. Thank you, Uncle Truby, for adopting and blessing our family. Now you and I should be a blessing to others.

# 58

## Mother Hen

"He shall cover thee with his feathers, and under his wings
shalt thou trust..." Psalm 91:4a (KJV)

I was only five years old when Hurricane Hazel hit our home. We
lived on a farm, and we had lots of chickens. The hurricane was
strong and destroyed some of our buildings. One of the buildings
destroyed was the henhouse. We walked outside after the storm,
and there were dead chickens everywhere. I helped Daddy pick up
the dead hens and bury them. Daddy picked up a dead hen and
under her wings were six baby chickens alive and well. She had
died protecting her babies. It reminded me of God giving His Life
for us. God tells us in Psalm 91:4 that He will cover you with his
feathers and that you can find refuge there. That was definitely a
God Moment!

# 59

## Macaroni and Cheese

"For God so loved the world that He gave His only begotten Son, that whoever believeth in Him should not perish, but have everlasting life." John 3:16 (KJV)

This story in the book called, *God Loves You Better Than Mac and Cheese.*

I have taught in several counties in North Carolina. One of the places I taught kindergarten was in Bladen County in a small, rural school. I had beautiful students who were mostly African Americans. One of my favorite students name was Billy Jack. Billy Jack was a chubby five-year-old who told me what he ate every meal and snack of the day.

One day Billy Jack looked at me and said, "Mrs. Rogers, me love you." I looked at Billy and said, "I love you, Billy Jack." He said, "No, Mrs. Rogers, you don't understand. Me love you." I thought maybe I didn't say it with as much feeling as he did. I stooped down and looked into Billy Jack's eyes and said, "Billy Jack, me love you, too." Billy smiled and said, "Mrs. Rogers, you don't understand; me love you better than broccoli, macaroni and cheese!" Now that is true love.

Did you know that Jesus loves you better than He loves mac and cheese? How much do you love him?

# 60

## A Hula-Hoop and A Bag of Candy

"Trust in the Lord and do good; so shalt thou dwell in the land and verily thou shalt be fed." Psalm 37:3 (KJV)

I had the best daddy in the whole world. He was tall, strong, gentle, and a Christian. He lived Jesus. He loved farming but didn't make enough money to pay the bills. He went to work as a plumber with the school system. Everyday Daddy would be home at exactly 5:30. Mama would have supper ready. All of us kids would watch at the door for him. When we saw him, we would all run out to greet him. Daddy would always bring us a treat, such as a bag of candy, sodas, or a balloon, and one time he brought us a hula-hoop. I know this was a sacrifice for Daddy because he didn't make much money at his job, but he always showed us love.

My earthly father's love reminds me of my Heavenly Father's love. Even if you do not have a good earthly father, you have an awesome Heavenly Father who loves you very much! My Heavenly Father sacrificed His life for us. I am so blessed to have had a daddy who loved God and his family. Thank you, both dads.

# 61

## Heavenly Sunflowers

"Then spake Jesus again unto them, saying, I am the light of the world; he that followeth me shall not walk in darkness, but shall have the light of life." John 8:12 (KJV)

One of my favorite flowers is the sunflower. I love its big, beautiful, happy, yellow face. My dad had been very sick in the hospital. We didn't know if he was going to live through the night. The next morning, the doctors said that they had lost his pulse during the night, but they had revived him. The next morning, Dad was sitting up in the bed smiling. I asked Dad what he had seen during the night. I told him, "Dad, you know you died last night, and God sent you back." He smiled and said, "I guess God is not finished with me yet. You know Heaven is real, and it is beautiful there. I was walking down a long lane, and on each side there were fields of sunflowers. Jesus was at the end of the lane. I was almost there when I was sent back."

I smiled. I believed it was God's way of telling us that Daddy was going to Heaven soon. I believe that the vision of the sunflowers was for me. Daddy did leave this earthly home exactly one month later, and I believe he walked that sunflower path to Jesus and to my mom. Thank you, God, for your assurance.

# 62

## Diapers from Heaven

"For the kingdom of God is not in word but in power." 1
Corinthians 4:20 (KJV)

One night at the pregnancy ministry a young Muslim woman came in and asked for a pack of size 4 diapers. I sat down across from her to counsel with her. She told me she did not want to hear anything about that Jesus stuff. She said, "I am Muslim, and I just came her for diapers." I asked her why she didn't go to a Muslim pregnancy center instead of a Christian one. She told me that there are not any Muslim pregnancy centers. I told her that we didn't have any size 4 diapers, but let's talk.

I started the conversation by asking her about her religious beliefs. I asked her what she had to do to go to Heaven. She gave me a long list of rules and sacrifices, and even if she followed them all, she wasn't sure of Heaven. I told her the steps to belief in Jesus: 1. Believe Jesus died on the cross for your sins. 2. Know that you are a sinner who needs a Savior. 3. Ask Jesus to come into your heart and life. I told her that I was absolutely sure that I was going to Heaven because of my relationship with Jesus. She listened. Finally she said, "If there is a real Jesus, then there will be a pack of size 4 diapers for me tonight." She was challenging God. I reminded her that there were not any size 4 diapers but that I would go and pray for some.

I went to the backroom and looked everywhere, hoping that there was a size 4 pack hiding somewhere.

I prayed, "God, show her who you are by providing a pack of size 4 diapers. God, please don't send size 3 diapers or size 5 diapers, just

4s." God whispered in my ear that He had saved me a pack of size 4 diapers at the back of a file cabinet that was in the storage room. I rushed over to the file cabinet, and there were the size 4 diapers. I praised God and ran back to the counseling room. I held up the size 4 diapers and said, "See, there is a real Jesus, and He just provided you with diapers for your baby." I wish you could have seen her face. She turned to leave and said, "I would like to know more about this Jesus." God is a creative God. If God sent manna from Heaven, then why not diapers?

# 63

## A Day to Remember

"A merry heart doeth good like a medicine..." Proverbs 17:22a (KJV)

I was blessed with five children; four of them are living. Before school would start, I would go to school early to prepare my kindergarten room for the new school year. One day I took all four children, plus my two nieces, to help get the room ready. The youngest child (name withheld to protect his manhood) messed up his diaper. I asked the two older children to take him to the bathroom and clean him up. They were gone awhile. Soon I heard laughing in the hall. I looked out, and they had the baby wrapped in a garbage bag hopping him down the hall. He looked stressed! I said, "What did you do to him?" They shared how they had taken him to the boys' bathroom (there were no other students at school) and tried to wash him off in the sink. The girls said it was a funny sink, and they couldn't get much water from the long sink. I thought, "Oh no, they put him in the urinal to clean him." Needless to say, we had to go home and give the youngest a bath. We still laugh at this memory, everyone that is, except the youngest. Are you making memories that will stand the test of time?

# 64

## A Child Shall Lead

"Whosoever therefore shall humble himself as this little child the same is the greatest in the kingdom of heaven."
Matthew 18:4 (KJV)

I work in crisis pregnancy centers as a counselor. One night I had a forty-six-year-old woman sitting in front of me. She had five children all with different dads. Her ten-year-old son had come in the counseling room with her. I talked with her about God and how Jesus had died for her. I told her of God's amazing love. Then I asked her if she wanted to accept Jesus. She said, "No, not today." Her ten-year-old son looked at her and said, "Mama, you need Jesus! Mama, you don't want Jesus, but I do. Can I ask Jesus into my heart?"

He closed his eyes and prayed the sinners' prayer. I gave him a Bible, and he was so happy. He whispered to me that he was going to work on his mom. Sometimes when we are witnessing to someone, we do not know who is listening. Share Jesus with everyone you meet as the Holy Spirit leads.

# Heart's Gold

"Jesus saith unto him, I am the way, the truth, and the life, no man cometh unto the Father, but by me." John 14:6 (KJV)

I was searching for a jewel of great value,
One worth far more than all the rest,
A priceless, sparkling gem,
The best of the best.

As my long and weary search for it continued,
I prayed for help from above,
And God's help came to me,
And I found my heart's love.

For the jewel of great value was really Jesus,
And He satisfied the need of my soul
I had found my heart's treasure,
Christ is its gold.

By Thomas Rogers

# 66

## Elevator Ministry

"Be not ye therefore like unto them, for your Father knoweth what things ye have need of, before you ask Him."
Matthew 6:8 (KJV)

I visit hospitals a lot taking baskets of clothes and baby items to newborn babies. Usually I load a little red wagon with basket layettes for new babies. I always pray that God will put someone on the elevator that needs to hear the Good News of Jesus. God always sends me someone. The elevator doors shut, and I ask the person if he knows Jesus. I press all the buttons so we will have more time to talk. Sometimes the elevator is slow, and we even have time for prayer.

One day I was waiting on the elevator to see who God would send that day. Three construction workers got on. I asked about Jesus. Two of the men knew Jesus. The other guy tried to leave out the back door. He was anxious to get away. When the door opened, he ran for the parking lot. The other two laughed and said, "Keep praying, Lady, we have been witnessing to him." Divine Appointments are all around us. Look for them.

# 67

## Meet Mr. Clarence

"And let us not be weary in well doing; for in due season we shall reap, if we faint not." Galatians 6:9 (KJV)

I taught in Rocky Mount, North Carolina. I was in a school with kids whose families were members of country clubs and kids from the low-income projects. I found that the common thread for all of these students was love. It was Christmas, and I was trying to teach my students about sharing God's love. We decided to adopt an elderly man who lived alone. This man was named Clarence. He was an old bachelor. His home was a run-down shack where all the animals ran in and out the open doors and windows. Mr. Clarence wore the same suit every Sunday. He smelled of moth balls. His job at the local church was to ring the bell. Clarence was always there early, always faithful.

The kindergarten class chose Mr. Clarence as their Christmas project. They made Christmas ornaments, made homemade cookies, and made Christmas cards, and everyone took Mr. Clarence a gift. Many of the affluent parents went with us as well. The children decorated Mr. Clarence's tree and gave him gifts and goodies. They thought he has the neatest house because all the animals were running in and out of the open doors and windows. There was even a goat on the table. The parents were in shock. The students brightened Mr. Clarence's Christmas. He said it was his best Christmas ever.

Mr. Clarence died six months later. The little Christmas tree was still up with all the handmade ornaments and cards. Twenty-seven years later, I still get cards from that class, and they speak of Mr. Clarence with love. We were all put here on this earth to make a difference in Jesus' name. The look in Mr. Clarence's eyes on that December day was definitely a God Moment.

# 68

## *Tractor*

"Blessed are the pure in heart, for they shall see God."
Matthew 5:8 (KJV)

Cole is my grandson, and he loves tractors. His first word was "tractor." He could name the different kinds of tractors when he was two years old. One day I said, "Cole, say John Deere." He said, "John Deere." "Cole, say Massey Ferguson." He said, "Ferguson." I said, "Cole, say International!" He looked at me and grinned and said, "Tractor." We all laughed. He couldn't say International, but he knew it was a tractor. Sometimes we might not know all the Jesus words to say, but it is important that we know Jesus.

# 69

## The Runaway

"He that followeth after righteousness and mercy findeth life, righteousness, and honour." Proverbs 21:21 (KJV)

I have taught kindergarten for forty years. One year I had a little boy named Scott. I had set him near the door because he was misbehaving. Scott decided it was time to go home, and he snuck out the door and walked three miles home. He parents thought it was funny. The principal didn't think it was funny; he punished Scott.

Later on that year, Scott hid under his bed for eight hours from his parents. They looked everywhere; they even started to drain the pond. Finally, Scott came out from under the bed. Needless to say, his parents didn't think it was funny this time. He was punished. As far as I know, that cured Scott from running away. We would save ourselves a lot of trouble if we would learn our lesson the first time.

# 70

## *"Holey" Car*

"I will praise thee, O Lord, among the people: I will sing unto thee among the nations." Psalm 57:9 (KJV)

I grew up on a farm in North Carolina. We were not rich in material things but wealthy in God's love. One of my favorite memories is our old car. The windows didn't work, and the doors had to be tied with a belt. The neatest thing about the car was that there was a big hole in the floor of the backseat. We loved the hole but had to be careful not to fall though. My sisters and I would sit on the seat and watch the road go by. We had the only car that had a floor roof instead of a sunroof. That car was the only one of its kind, unique.

Sometimes it is not the biggest or best things that make good memories. Memories are what we make them to be. Others may have seen the car as a bad memory, but to the three little girls it was lots of wonderful memories.

# 71

## Kassi's Letter

"Lo, children are a heritage of the Lord..." Psalm 127:3 (KJV)

Dear People,

Who would want to kill innocent babies? Abortion is the murder of a little baby that is growing inside of its mama. I believe it is wrong to kill babies.

God doesn't like abortions. It says so in the Bible. Jeremiah 1:5, God said, "Before I formed you in the womb I knew you."

God has special plans for each and everyone of us.

Babies deserve to live. They have as much right as big people do. They should be loved. Instead of killing your baby you should put your baby up for adoption.

Abortion kills the baby and hurts the Mom. The baby can feel pain. The mother will one day realize that she killed her baby and she will be very sad.

How do you feel about abortion? I hope you can see that abortion is very wrong. Please help save the babies. I will be walking in the Walk for Life, will you? Love Kassidy Nixon, 10 years old

Kassi, my granddaughter, wrote this when she was ten years old. God tells us that we can learn much from children. If a child can see abortion as murder, then why can't adults.

# 72

## Mother Teresa

"Lo, children are a heritage of the Lord..." Psalm 127:3 (KJV)

Mother Teresa of Calcutta spoke words at the National Prayer Breakfast on February 3rd, 1994. She spoke boldly and without apology.

"But I feel the greatest destroyer of peace today is abortion, because it is a war against the child, a direct killing of the innocent child, murder by the mother herself. And if we accept that a mother can kill her own child, how can we tell other people not to kill one another. By abortion, the mother does not learn to love, but kills her own child to solve her problems. And by abortion, that father is told that he does not have any responsibility at all for the child he has brought into the world. The father is likely to put other women into the same trouble, so abortion just leads to other abortions. Any country that accepts abortion is not teaching its people to love, but to use any violence to get what they want. This is why the greatest destroyer of peace and love is abortion."

Mother Teresa also said, "How can there be too many children? That is like saying there are too many flowers."

# 73

## *First Plane Trip*

"And the Lord, he it is doth go before thee, he will go with me, he will not fail thee." Deuteronomy 31:8a (KJV)

I try to be obedient to God. I have never had a desire to fly in a plane. One day this past year a lady asked me to speak in Smithville, Texas, for a new maternity home banquet. The transportation to get to Texas was a plane. I was nervous but trusted God to care for me. I boarded the plane. There was a little two year old girl in front of me. She said "This is my first airplane ride." I echoed her statement. Later on the stewardess brought the little girl and me a flight wing pin.

Everywhere God had me on the plane and at the conference, he placed people in my path to share Jesus with. We had to change planes in Texas. There was a man who had a ticket for the middle of the plane. He decided he wanted to move back. Every time he would move to another seat, someone would get on with that ticket. I watched God move this man all the way to the back of the plane where I was sitting. He was a successful real estate man who was purchasing a home in the Bahamas. I asked him about Jesus. He didn't know Jesus, but he told me about being adopted when he was born. His mother was only sixteen years old when he was born. My friends said, "Helen, did you notice the plane leaned as you talked to the man?" The other passengers were listening to the conversation. God is so good. Divine Appointments are everywhere.

Another person I met was in the airport bathroom. There was a bathroom attendant standing there. I smiled at her and asked her if she would like one of my books, *God Loves You Better Than Mac and Cheese*. She started crying and took out two pictures of her daughters, Maria and Amanda. Maria was six, and Amanda was eight. Both of her daughters had died within two months of each other with a deadly disease. She was hurting and missing her daughters. I asked if I could pray for her. All four of us gathered around Ruth and prayed for her right there in the airport bathroom.

I found that God will ask us to do unusual things to bless others. God knew that lady needed a human touch of God. The funny thing to me is that there are thousands of people every day in the airport who are lonely and lost. Everyone seems to focus on self only. Let's look around for the Divine Appointments God has placed in our path.

# 74

## Offering Plate

"For as many as are led by the Spirit of God, they are the sons of God." Romans 8:14 (KJV)

I heard a story of a little boy who had never been to church. The neighborhood church had a bus ministry, so the little boy went to Sunday school. He loved the songs and stories about Jesus. This little boy didn't know much about love in his own home. He liked the feeling of being loved and accepted. He sat with the bus driver during big church. He saw the offering plate coming. He said, "Mister, what they doing?" The man explained that they were taking up money so that people would know of Jesus' love.

The little boy wanted to give something to Jesus. He dug deep in his pockets. All he could find was a rock, a bird feather, a marble, a nail, and some lint. He wanted so desperately to give something to Jesus. He got an idea. He ran to the back of the church where the offering plate was on the last row. He took the offering plate, placed it on the floor, and stood in the middle of the plate. His words were "Jesus, all I have to give you is myself."

Isn't that the most important thing to Christ? Jesus wants us to totally give ourselves to Him. He is able to use it to accomplish mighty deeds for the kingdom.

# 75

## "Modern-Day" Proverbs Women

"Many daughters have done virtuously, but thou excellest them all." Proverbs 31:29 (KJV)

This is a revision of the Proverbs 31 woman. I placed this in my first book, *God Loves You Better Than Mac and Cheese.*

I love the scripture of the Proverbs 31 woman. I rewrote it for the modern-day woman.

A wife of unique character who can find? She is worth far more that stocks and IRAs. Her husband wonders about her sanity and still smiles. She brings him laughter and joy all the days of his life. She buys Wal-Mart specials and clips coupons to save every cent she can. She is like a merchant ship bringing her food from McDonalds and KFC. She gets up while it is still dark to pack lunches and to lay out clothes for her family for the day. She considers a yard sale and buys unique stuff. Out of her money she gives each child his allowance and gives the rest to someone in need. She is a taxi driver, getting each and every one of her children to the ball practices, dance recitals, and church functions while still keeping up with all the homework, cooking, cleaning, and shopping.

She sets about her work tired from the day before. Her heart aches for the wayward child as her knees bend many times to petition God for the needs of her family. She knows a good deal at the local store and will be there two hours early before it is gone. Her light is the last to go out at night after she has checked the doors, the stove, and the heat. She goes into her children's room to make sure all is well. Her last stop is the Bible to read and pray for God's protection on her family. She praises God for all His blessings. In her hand she holds a list of things to be done, with a small child pulling at her leg to go outside and pick dandelions. She gives all her birthday money to a child in need and stretches out her heart and home to the hurting.

When it snows, she clothes her children in warm coats, scarves, and mittens and starts a snowball fight. Later she will make snow cream with them as they laugh and remember their snowy day. She has happy face pillows and sheets. Her husband is pitied at the local diner where he does to get a cup of coffee as he shares his wife's latest adventures. She makes cookbooks and sells them to fund her kindergarten beach trip. She is clothed in clown suits, den mother outfits, and hand-me-down clothes and lots of love. She smiles at the day's end, asking God to forgive her for the things she didn't get done.

She speaks with motherly authority, mostly saying, "Do it because I said so!" She vacuums the floors, washes mountains of clothes, feeds the endless pits of hunger, does mission work, and often forgets to eat herself. Her children rise up and call her again, again, and again! Her husband calls her, too. Have you seen my car keys, my reading book, or my glasses? I left that important paper on the dining room table two weeks ago. Did you move it? Many woman work two jobs, but you have three. Charm is not on your list. Beauty is not found in jars of makeup. A woman who loves her husband and her children will leave a legacy that will stand the test of time. "A hundred years from now, it will not matter how clean my house was or if all the laundry was done. What will be important is that I gave my husband and children love, laughter, happy memories, and a firm foundation in the Lord. My gift for them is legacy of Jesus."

# 76

## *The Beautician*

"Before the mountains were born or you brought forth the earth and the world, from everlasting to everlasting you are God." Psalm 90:2 (KJV)

I was the oldest of four children, and I was a very mischievous child. Mom and Dad would leave me at the house with my brother and sisters while they would go to work in the fields. One day I found a pair of scissors and decided I wanted to be a beautician. I cut all the hair off my dolls and I cut all the hair off my white puppy. I needed more victims; I mean more clients. So I cornered my sisters. I cut their hair. When Mom and Dad came in from the field, there was hair everywhere. Needless to say, Mom and Dad took my scissors away and gave the beautician a spanking.

Every time I pick up a pair of scissors, I am reminded of my sin. How many times do we sin when we know our parents are away? It is the same with us and God. We think God is not looking, and we do our sins. God is always here with you; there is no hiding of sins from God, and there are consequences.

# 77

## *The Bible*

"With long life will I satisfy him, and show him my salvation." Psalm 91:16 (KJV)

I was teaching at a Christian school near my home. I had a beautiful student named Hailey who loved Jesus with all her heart. Each morning she would go to the lunchroom for breakfast where the public school students were waiting for the school bus. She made friends with a little boy named Ben. Every morning Hailey would talk to Ben about Jesus. One morning she met me at the door and said, "Mrs. Rogers, can I bring Ben a Bible? He loves Jesus, but his family doesn't." I told her that would be great.

I called Hailey's mom to tell her about Hailey's desire to give a Bible to Ben. She said she would let Hailey choose one of her Bibles for Ben. The next day when I came to the lunchroom, Hailey was sitting with Ben, and they were reading the Bible together.

Hailey had given Ben her favorite easy-reader Bible. Hailey's heart is filled with Jesus, and it overflows to all she meets. She is a five-year-old missionary. We as adults need to be like Hailey. Hailey was obedient to God, and Ben was blessed by her.

## Twenty Dollars

"I love them that love me, and those that seek me early shall find me." Proverbs 8:17 (KJV)

I have taught kindergarten for forty years. This past year, I had a boy in my class named Kel. We had a program at school, and all the parents and grandparents came to watch the student program. The next day after the program, Kel walked in the room with a twenty-dollar bill in an empty potato chip bag. I asked Kel what the twenty dollars was for. He said, "I did good at the program last night, and Grandpa gave me twenty dollars. I don't need anything, so you can use the twenty dollars for the babies that you help." I love children. They remind me of the goodness of God.

# 79

## Living/Nonliving

"Let the words of my mouth, and the meditation of my heart, be acceptable in thy sight, O Lord, my strength, my redeemer." Psalm 29:14 (KJV)

I love my kindergarten children. I was teaching a science lesson on living and nonliving things. I had taught the story of Jesus' death on the cross and His resurrection. All the students cheered that Jesus was not dead but alive.

That day during science, I asked the students to draw five living things and five nonliving things. Hailey brought me her paper. She had drawn a toy, chalk, a car, a chair, and a bed for her nonliving things. Living things were Mom, Dad, herself, her puppy, and there was one more picture. Hailey said, "Mrs. Rogers, this is a picture of Jesus. I put Him under living."

Praise God! She had it! Jesus is alive and will love us forever.

# 80

## Prayer Answered

"But my God shall supply all your need according to his riches in glory by Christ Jesus." Philippians 4:19 (KJV)

I was working with a homeless family at the pregnancy center. We were trying to help them move from a condemned home. We don't have money to do that in our budget. I went to the post office, and there was an unexpected check for one thousand dollars from the homeless coalition. I smiled and thanked God. He always has what we need, especially when we are helping others. God is always on time and meets all our needs.

# 81

## *Baby Saved*

"He will cover you with his feathers, and under his wings you will find refuge…" Psalm 91:4 (KJV)

I have a client who has a beautiful, little boy named Henry. Henry is one year old now and has beautiful curly hair. His mom is a good mother and has recently fought cancer. When Henry was born, he had to wear a brace. They waited to do his circumcision until after he got his brace off. Mom took Henry to the doctor, and they did his circumcision. She brought him home and put him to bed. Mom usually checked on him at 6:00 a.m. each morning. God woke her up at 4:00 a.m. and told her to check on Henry. She went to him, and he had pulled his stitches out. There was blood everywhere. She carried him to the ER. The doctor said that if she had not gotten to him in time, then he would have bled out.

God blessed Henry by protecting his life. God has a special plan for Henry. He has a special plan for you, too.

# 82

## Kindergarten Homework

"Blessed is he that considereth the poor, the Lord will deliver him in times of trouble." Psalm 41:1 (KJV)

I taught kindergarten in Rocky Mount about nineteen years ago and then we moved to Fayetteville. This spring, I was invited to a wedding tea party for one of my former students from Rocky Mount named Lauren. Her grandmother wanted to surprise Lauren by inviting me. I went to the tea, and Lauren was glad to see me. She is a beautiful, young, Christian woman who is helping with counseling sessions for women in need. Her mother told me that after I left Rocky Mount that Lauren would look for me hoping I had moved back to Rocky Mount. Lauren's Mom reminded me of a particular assignment that I gave Lauren in kindergarten that had planted a seed.

I had given all the students the assignment to pick one country and then share with the class. Lauren chose Mexico. Lauren finished high school, studied Spanish, and got her psychology degree. God used the seed that was planted about Mexico in kindergarten. She went to Mexico and worked as a director of a Christian, Spanish orphanage. We do not know the seeds we plant as we walk through this life. Walk in the footsteps of Jesus because someone is following in your footsteps.

# 83

## *Divine Appointment*

"God be merciful unto us, and bless us; and cause His face to shine upon us." Psalm 67:1 (KJV)

Keith, a fifteen-year-old, came to the pregnancy center to volunteer one night. I knew he was Hindu. He helped with the food bags and clothes. The night ended; I took Keith aside and shared with him about Jesus. I asked him what he knew about Jesus. I challenged him to read the Bible. He accepted Jesus that night. I prayed for Keith because I knew he would have a hard time going home to Hindu parents. Keith rode home with a volunteer. Keith kept saying, "I am so full, so happy, that Jesus is in my heart, and I want to live for Him." We are to share Jesus with all we meet. His parents told him it was his decision. Pray that he will lead his family to Christ.

# 84

## Listen to the Lord

"My little children, let us not love in word, neither in tongue; but in deed and in truth." 1 John 3:18 (KJV)

Ed and I got married on a hot summer day in August. We didn't have any money for a honeymoon, my Daddy gave us $40 for a night in a hotel in Raleigh. The next morning we got up at 7:00 and drove 70 miles to our new church that we would be attending as Mr. and Mrs.

Ed was a teacher at a local high school and I worked in an elementary school as a librarian. Ed and I had talked about having children one day. We had been married two months. One day at the school where I was working, there was a little boy who was being taken away from his parents. There was no one to take this child, he had no relatives. I took one look at this precious boy and I felt the Holy Spirit prompt me to call Ed. I asked Ed, "Would you like to be a father?" He said, "Yes, sometime in the future." I said, "What about tonight?" He sounded shock and then he said, "Did you forget to tell me something?" I shared with him about the little boy who needed a home. We brought this little boy home with us. He stayed with us for one year the first year of our marriage. This gave his mom and dad time to get cleaned up so they could get their children back. Ed and I learned a lot that first year. God blessed us. We didn't know that God was preparing us for more foster children and five children of our own. Our home was always full of children. We were blessed by them all.

# 85

## *God Forgives*

"And the prayer of faith shall save the sick, and the Lord shall raise him up; and if he have committed sins, they shall be forgiven him." James 5:15 (KJV)

I had a kindergarten mom that would avoid me. She wouldn't even look at me. I continued to try to reach out to this mom but to no avail. The year ended, and we had a program for all the parents. I shared my book, <u>God Loves You Better Than Mac and Cheese</u> with all my parents, even Linda. Linda took the book. This book is a book of miracles that I have seen in pregnancy ministries over twenty-six years. I got a call from Linda the next day. She said she had read the book in one night. She apologized for being so cold toward me for the year. She started crying as she shared her story. Linda said, "Every time I looked at you, I was reminded of what you stood for. I know you leave school and work in ministries that save babies from abortions. I am a nurse, and I aborted my baby three years ago. God can never forgive me." I reassured her that God could and would forgive her for the abortion. We prayed and then I knew why God had placed me at this school for such a time as this. God will place us where we are needed to be the hands, feet, and heart of Jesus.

# 86

## Pray For My Dad

"In him was life, and the life was the light of men." John 1:4 (KJV)

I worked at a Christian school for five years. Each morning I would share a Bible story. I shared the Easter story that particular morning. The Holy Spirit was so strong in our room. One of my students prayed to accept Jesus. He prayed the sinners' prayer, and all the other students cheered. Sam's prayer request each day after that was for his dad to come to know Jesus. We had our end of the year awards program. I knew this would be a good opportunity to witness to Sam's dad.

I walked over to Sam's dad, Ben, and said, "Ben, I need to know if Jesus is your Lord and Savior." Tears came into his eyes, and he said, "Mrs. Rogers, because of you, I have accepted Jesus." Sam was standing near his dad and hugged him because he had heard the conversation. I heard on Monday that Ben and his whole family were in church on Sunday.

Please pray for Sam. His dad has strayed and left his family. Sam continues to pray for his dad. I believe God will hear and answer this child's prayer.

# 87

## Happy Face Shirts

"Delight thyself also in the Lord, and he shall give thee the desires of thine heart." Psalm 37:4

My kindergarten class was going on a field trip. I wanted to order shirts for the class trip. I decided to order yellow shirts with one big happy face on the front and small happy faces around the big one. I had "Mrs. Roger's Little Joys" put on the shirt. They sent me a sample of what the yellow shirts would look like. There was another sample of purple shirts with happy faces. I had a hard time deciding which one I wanted. I only had enough money for one set. I chose the yellow shirts but whispered a prayer to the Lord that he would bless me with the purple shirts, too. My friend Rose walked in and said, "Mrs. Rogers, have you been praying?" The company had made a mistake; they did the yellow shirts and the purple ones by accident. They sent me both sets with no charge for the purple ones. I smiled. God is wonderful, and this was definitely a God Moment.

# 88

## *Not A Good Idea*

"Bear ye one another's burdens, and so fulfil the law of Christ." Galatians 6:2 (KJV)

I had never been on an airplane before, and I did not know all the airport rules. I got tired of carrying my bag, so I decided to put my luggage bag on the escalator and to let it ride to the top. It sounded like a good idea to me! I put the bags on the escalator, and my friend caught them at the top. All of a sudden, we heard a loud whistle, and a man came out with SWAT gear on. I said to my friends, "Somebody is in trouble!" Guess who the somebody was? It was me. I didn't know you could not leave your baggage. He told us we must have our baggage in our hands at all times. I called my husband. He asked me to please not get arrested in Texas as he was in North Carolina.

Sometimes we learn the hard way. I know now that airports have lots of rules. Next time I fly, I will learn the rules ahead of time.

# 89

## Crazy White Lady

"For the kingdom of God is not in word, but in power." 1
Corinthians 4:20

I met a pastor from South Africa. He was fascinated with the
pregnancy ministry. He looked at me one day and said, "You need
to come to South Africa and start a pregnancy ministry." I smiled
and said, "I have to do these here in the USA." A little later on, he
saw me dressed in a clown suit ministering to children. He said,
"You come to South Africa and make my children laugh." I told him,
"They wouldn't know what to do with this crazy, white woman." He
smiled and said, "You come to South Africa. We put up big sign that
say come see crazy white woman. When they come, we tell them all
about Jesus." God uses many ways to get His word out.

# 90

## Forty Years Old

"And we know that all things work together for good to them that love God, to them who are the called according to his purpose." Romans 8:28 (KJV)

Joan is a forty-year-old, and she called to ask for an abortion at the pregnancy center. She said that her children were all grown and that she was too old to have a baby. She wanted an abortion, and I told her we didn't do abortions. I asked her to please come to see me. She said she had a Saturday appointment at the abortion clinic. I told her I would pray that she didn't keep the appointment.

I called her Saturday afternoon, and she had not gotten the abortion. She promised she would come to see me at the center. Joan came, and we talked about God's special plans for this little one. She is a nursing assistant, and money is tight. I asked how she was going to pay for the abortion, and she said that the abortion clinic offered her a free scholarship to kill her baby. We talked and prayed together. She agreed to come in for a free ultrasound the next week. She did come, and she saw her baby boy bouncing around in the womb. I referred her to a pro-life doctor. She said the doctor was kind and hugged her for choosing life. Joan is excited about her son whom the Lord has blessed her with. Many times we think something is bad, but God can bring good out of it. Please pray for Joan and her baby.

# 91

## Raped and Hurting

"And we know that all things work together for good to them that love God…" Romans 8:28a (KJV)

Lisa is a fourteen-year-old. She called the center and asked for an abortion. I counseled with her and asked her to come in. Lisa was not sure what to do. She told me that she was keeping herself until marriage, but this man came to her house and molested her sister and raped her. Now she was pregnant, and she had to make a choice. She thought about adoption. We gave her a free ultrasound. She told me if she was going to have a girl, then she would parent the baby. She didn't want a boy because she felt he would look like the man who had raped her. She went into the ultrasound room and came out clutching the pictures. I asked her what she was having. She smiled and said "a boy." Lisa said, "Miss Helen, I'm going to parent my baby." She had fallen in love with her little one in the womb. It will be hard for Lisa, but I believe with all my heart that this baby will help her heal. The father sinned, not the baby. Lisa is a good mother; her mom helps her. Lisa goes to school and plans to go to college.

I told Lisa that in God's eyes, she is still a virgin. She is waiting for the husband God wants her to have. The man who raped her had also raped his own two daughters and two other girls. The police are looking for him. Please pray he will be caught so he will not hurt other young girls.

# 92

## Debt Forgiven

"But my God shall supply your needs according to his riches in glory by Christ Jesus." Philippians 4:19 (KJV)

We have been going to the same family dentist for many years. I have taught all his children in kindergarten. They are good, kind, godly people. The daddy is now semi-retired, and his son is now the dentist. It is funny; I used to sit beside him and read the Tooth Book in kindergarten, now he is my dentist. Our dental bill was high. We have never had dental insurance. I would pay one hundred dollars each month to pay down the $2400 bill. I received a letter in the mail from the dentist. I thought it was a bill from the dentist. I opened the letter, and there was my check returned. The bill said, "God is good. Thank you for all you do." The amount I owed was a zero dollar balance. They had forgiven $2400; God is good!

God is in the blessing business. This kind of deed was a much needed blessing as I was struggling to pay some medical bills. We serve a mighty God. That definitely was a God Moment. I think about Jesus dying for me and writing a pardon for my sins. It says "paid in full."

# 93

## Blown Fuse

"In everything give thanks, for this is the will of God in Christ Jesus concerning you." 1 Thessalonians 5:18 (KJV)

I have a grandson named Cole. He is three years old. He has a small four-wheeler, and he loves to ride it. One day he left it in the rain. This caused the four-wheeler to not go in reverse. Papa Ed was checking it out to see why the four-wheeler was having trouble. He told Cole it might be several problems. Cole and Papa Ed got the tools and started checking. He looked over at Cole, and he was blowing on a fuse. Ed said, "Cole, what are you doing?" He said, "Papa Ed, you said it might be a blown fuse, so I'm blowing on the fuse." How many times do we take things literally?

# 94

## *Yard Sale*

"Rejoice always, pray without ceasing..." 1 Thessalonians 5:16 (KJV)

My granddaughters and I were having a yard sale. I had cleaned out my closet and had twenty dresses in size twenty-four that I was selling. We set up the yard sale. I looked up to the sky and said, "Lord, please send a lady to buy all these dresses." My granddaughters laughed. Ten minutes later a lady stopped and bought all the dresses. Heidi and Kassi said that God sure answered that prayer quickly. We have not because we asked not. God does and will answer all prayers.

# 95

## Daddy, Help Me

"Behold, I will do a new thing, now it shall spring forth; shall he not know it? I will even make a way in the wilderness, and rivers in the desert." Isaiah 43:19 (KJV)

I had a young lady come by the center to volunteer. She was fifteen years old. She shared her story with me. Gabby told me that when she was five years old, her dad left. Her mom remarried. Her stepdad started molesting her when she was six. It went on for many years. Gabby became hard and started running with the wrong crowd. She started drinking, doing drugs, and cutting herself.

Gabby's daddy came back into her life. He confessed that he had come to the house when Gabby was six and had seen her stepfather molesting her. He did nothing; he walked away. Gabby said, "Daddy, why didn't you help me?" Gabby's life continued to go downhill.

One summer she went to a Christian camp and got saved. She stood in front of me with tears in her eyes. She said, "Miss Helen, I have forgiven my stepdad and dad. My Heavenly Father has helped me. I am a child of the Most High King. I am a princess. I believe God is going to use these bad things in my life to help others. I am healed."

# 96

## *"The Sunset"*

"Be still and know that I am God…" Psalm 46:10 (KJV)

God creates a work of art each end of the day.
Each work has a different touch in a special way.
With the sky as His canvas spacious and new,
He creates a masterpiece with a touch of dew.
God takes His paintbrush and touches the sky.
His breath pushes the stormy clouds and makes them just go by.
A splash of golden sunshine, and a touch of baby blue.
Tiny little patches with a pinkish hue.
Only light colors signify the cheer and happiness,
As they are spread across the sky.
So thank God for blessing you all the day.
And watch his masterpiece at the end of the day.

By Dawn Rogers "92"

# 97

## "Why"

"Ye are the light of the world…" Matthew 5:14 (KJV)

On the street I saw a young, pregnant teen, scared and alone in an abortion world with little hope for her and her precious baby. I became angry and said to God, "Why don't you do something about it?" For a while, God said nothing. That night He replied, "I certainly did something about it. I made YOU!"

Helen Rogers

# 98

## Special Flowers

"Rejoice in the Lord, O ye righteous for praise is comely for the upright." Psalm 33:1 (KJV)

Last week I was at the center; it had been an extremely hard day in ministry. There were so many women with needs. That day had brought a woman who was being abused by her husband, and she and the children had left him. A young woman had called and asked for an abortion. You could hear a little baby crying in the background. Another woman came by to learn how to control her anger. Her life was full of pain and suffering. Another young woman called and asked for help. She had three children; they were one, three, and five years old. Her husband had deserted her. She had one small pack of chicken in the refrigerator and a cup of milk. There was no more food in the house. She had a little heater to keep warm, but the kerosene was running low. Her children were sleeping in a chair. She had three chairs and a mattress on the floor. Her dishes included three bowls, three spoons, and a crock pot. One towel and a wash cloth was all she had. There was no furniture. She had moved to this area, and there was no one to help her. She called the center and asked for food and clothes. She didn't know anyone so she called a help line, and someone had told her to try to call the center. We took food, clothes, dishes, furniture, beds, toys, and other items. She wept for joy.

That night as I was finishing up the day, I was extremely tired and discouraged. A man came to the door of the center with a bouquet of flowers in his hand. He said, "I was in Wal-Mart, and

God told me to bring the beautiful lady who helps moms and babies flowers." He said these flowers are from God. I cried as I took the flowers. God, you do know, and you do care. Thank you for encouraging me and giving me strength to continue on. Do you know those flowers lasted longer and stayed fresher than any other cut flowers I have ever had? Thank you, God, for the flowers.

## Ten Days

"For we walk by faith, not by sight." 2 Corinthians 5:7 (KJV)

I have worked with crisis pregnancy centers for twenty-six years. In the pregnancy ministry, we walk entirely by faith. God supplies all the needs of the center. This past December, the expenses were heavy, and the bank account for the center was low. I try to pay all ministry bills on time, as that honors God. We had three insurances come due at the same time. All the rents for the four ministries were due, along with the regular bills. I went to God, and I said, "Thank you, God, for providing." He told me to write newsletters and share the needs of the center. I sent the newsletter, and I saw God move on His people. God sent $20,000 in ten days. The wonderful thing is that God sent it in many different amounts. I praise God for being an on time God. That was definitely a God Moment.

# 100

## Will You Take My Baby?

"Lo children are a heritage of the Lord; and the fruit of the womb is his reward." Psalm 127:3 (KJV)

One of our crisis centers is right across the street from an abortion clinic. We had a young woman to leave the abortion clinic and come to us. She said she was too far along to get an abortion. She was planning to go to Chapel Hill to get the abortion. We talked and prayed. She still was not sure of her decision. I called her and she was still planning on getting an abortion. I texted her and told her to please carry the baby. I would adopt the baby. She called later and asked me to take the baby. I told her I would but that I am 65 years old. I could help her find a younger family for her baby. She said, "I want you" I told her we would keep praying. God has worked out every detail. She called me and she is keeping her precious little boy who is due in August. She said, "I am trusting God to provide for my family." God will provide and she will never regret her decision for life.

# 101

## *Here's Your Sign*

"For the kingdom of God is not in word but in power." 1
Corinthians 4:20 "(KJV)

My husband and I were on the way to the crisis center one Saturday
morning. We drive a van with life signs on the doors. An elderly
man walked over to our door and said "What do you do at that
place?" He was pointed to the sign on the door. We told him that
we helped Moms choose life for their babies. He handed me a phone
number and said "Call my niece, she is going to get an abortion this
morning." I called and I could not get an answer. I texted her and
told her to please not kill her baby. There are many ways that we
can help at the center. I shared with her that the baby was innocent
and a blessing from God. She called and she had read the text and
decided not to do the abortion. She agreed to come in and get a free
ultra-sound. She came and saw her little one jumping around in the
womb. She chose life. She shared with me that the father of the baby
had died in a car wreck two weeks ago. She felt hopeless with no way
to turn. She chose life and the little one is due in August. She just
needed to see Jesus with Hope. We are to be Jesus- with- skin-on. PS
Amy left us after the ultrasound and went home. Someone gave her
the money to get an abortion and told her that was her best choice.
I called to check on Amy and she was sad and depressed. She had
just gotten an abortion and had lots of regrets for her choice. We will
walk her through this valley and God will heal her. I have never met
a woman who was glad she killed her baby.

# 102
## *What Do You Treasure?*

"Delight yourself in the Lord and He shall give thee the desires of thine heart." Psalm 37:4

I taught kindergarten for forty years. I was teaching in Rocky Mount and I had a student to register for kindergarten. He was from Kuwait and his Daddy was killed during the war. His Mom moved to America to protect her children. Tareq loved living in America. Our class gave him a welcome to America party. The students bought in toys, books, clothes, and lots of items. One of the items that Tareq got was a small American flag. He treasured that flag and carried it in his booksack every day. Tareq realized even at a young age that freedom was a heart's desire. So many times we take our freedom in America for granted and we also take our freedom in Christ for granted. Freedom is not free. It costs Christ His life.

# Biography

Helen McLeod Rogers lives in Lillington, North Carolina. She has been married to Rev. Ed Rogers for forty-five years. They have six children and five precious grandchildren. Helen has a master's degree in early childhood education and has retired from teaching kindergarten after forty years.

Twenty-six years ago, Helen took a stand for life. Since that time, she and her husband have started several pregnancy ministries in North Carolina. They have recently added a new pregnancy ministry in Columbia called Jesus Loves the Little Children. God Loves You Better Than Mac and Cheese was Helen's first book, and God has ordained this one called That's Such a God Thing.

Printed in the United States
By Bookmasters